Ghost Lite

Ghost Lite

J. Elliott

Hedonistic Hound Press

Acknowledgements

I am privileged to have had two review teams whose kindness, encouragement and insightful critiques have been invaluable. Thank you to Skipper, Richard, Pat, Kim and Catherine of the Writer's Alliance of Gainesville. Many thanks also to the Writer's Group of the Alachua Branch Library: Joanne, Art, Fran, Betty, Jacqui and Peggy. Having dedicated and honest cheerleaders is invaluable. Many blessings and much success to you all, always.

*Many thanks to Rohan for being a sounding board, to Laurel and Chip for spot-on editing, and Linda for help with elevator protocol. Sharon and Wendy, thank you for technical support with **dpi** and talking me out of the trees!*

Special thanks to Rick for your love, encouragement and support. I could not have done this without you.

Jessica Elliott   2016

Table of Contents

Note

I know it's tacky as all get out to toot my own horn, but I love this story. It has taken twenty-five years to get it published, first appearing in Volume Three of Grey Matter, A Science Fiction Fantasy Digest published by Aaron Meizius. It launched all the others.

The idea came about while I was working reception at a doctor's office and the nurses were talking about a woman with schizophrenia who claimed to have entities in her house. I couldn't stop wondering, "what if her house really was haunted and no one believed her?"

An Old House Just Has So Much Character

The plump woman looked up from her flower bed and waved, "Yoo-hoo! Hello! Oh, let me catch my breath, I was just trying to get some new annuals in the beds you know, it always looks so bleak this time of year. I wanted some color, but the weeds are tenacious, aren't they, even after the frosts? Whew! Well hello, I'm Lucy Peabody. You must be the new neighbor."

The young man approached her and the two shook hands.

"I saw the moving van and said, 'Oh good, new neighbors at last.' A house hates to be empty, you know, always looks so forlorn, why, I'm sure you'll bring it back to life in no time. Are you married? My husband passed away ten years ago, and I've just stayed on, don't know what else to do -- I do love it here, but it's a bit much for me anymore. I'll be so glad to have someone next door again."

"Thank you, I—" the man said, distracted by the bun on Mrs. Peabody's head that jiggled as she talked.

"You know, Mr. Johnson moved away right after Mrs. Johnson died, and the house has been alone for a while now, although that perky real estate lady trooped over here all the time. Never stayed long though. I bet you love old houses, don't you? They just have so much character, and yours, why, it's quite something with that grand staircase, and all that old wood. Of course, the front porch'll need a bit of work, but really, it's a solid house."

"Yes, I—" the new neighbor said.

"So sad about Peggy Johnson you know, I don't think it was a good fit for the Johnsons. He was away on business so much, and she wasn't well. He really should've spent more time at home. She was a very nervous person, and you know I don't like gossip, but she did say that she kept seeing the doctors about her disorder. She was schizophrenic -- bi-polar – something like that." Mrs. Peabody flapped a hand dismissively.

"She had good days and bad days, why sometimes we'd have tea together and a really nice chat and it'd be all right, and then sometimes she seemed so agitated, almost frightened and she'd say that she was having trouble with the doctors getting her medications straight."

Mrs. Peabody aimed the trowel at the man. "Her husband didn't seem to have much patience with her, and he was gone so much. You know it really gave me the creeps the way she'd say she heard dreadful noises at all hours, and voices, angry voices telling her all kinds of weird things. She swore sometimes there were messages written on the wall telling her to get out and that she was going to *die* – can you believe it? Then the doctors would adjust her prescriptions and she'd be calmer. Nowadays there's a pill for everything, right? Why just the other day I was in a café downtown and these ladies were comparing their medications like they were swapping recipes! I don't go for it, myself, no sir-ee. I'm fit as a fiddle. Commercials go on 'try the blue pill' like it'd be a treat. Then they list the side effects. Nonsense!"

"And you know, poor Peggy was so fragile. She said she was part Cherokee Indian, and her grandmother used to have premonitions and see apparitions. A seer, Peggy said. Folks would go to her granny for advice. Whenever someone in the family passed on, they'd appear to her granny like they were saying goodbye in a gentle way. Just show up next to her bed, and then disappear.

Sometimes I think Peggy saw things too, I do." She put her hands on her hips.

"Why, there was that one time she scared me half to death, running over here wild-eyed in her nightgown and crying that she just couldn't stay in that house with the banging in the walls and something trying to kill her. Said something shoved her and pulled the little kitchen rug out from under her to make her fall, she almost burned herself real bad on the stove, but fortunately, she caught herself by grabbing the freezer door as she went down. She got a nasty burn on her elbow. Guess it could've been lots worse. Poor thing, probably the medication making her fuzzy-headed and confused. She probably had her head down rummaging in the fridge and got dizzy."

Mrs. Peabody flipped the trowel around and tapped the handle in her open palm like a gavel. "I declare, she got herself into such a state, I let her stay here that night on the couch. When I woke up in the morning she was gone. I think she was embarrassed about how she'd gotten carried away in her mind, you know. Her all alone in that big old house, I'm sure her imagination got the best of her sometimes. Then her husband would be back for a while, and I didn't see much of her. I even stopped over, and he'd say Peggy was not well and was resting."

"How — ?" the man began.

"They could have done something with that house, but what with him gone and her so frail, they didn't get around to much. The poor thing was so lonely and isolated. She didn't go out hardly at all. Oh, they went out to dinner a few times, I saw them drive into town together on occasion, but I know she was lonely. Other than me she didn't have anyone to talk to. Mr. and Mrs. Hoskins over in that house, hardly ever come out –they're kind of recluses, they are, and what with being in this cul-de-sac, kind of separate back here in the trees, well, we don't see many of the other folks up the street much. They walk the other way when they go for walks."

She pointed the trowel handle at him. "Peggy did like her potted plants, though. Geraniums, she loved geraniums. She did try to make the house look cheerier. Funny, she used to be all scratched up on her arms, you know? She said it was the plantings, but that didn't really make sense—she wasn't planting roses or anything really thorny, and she didn't have a cat either, so I didn't know what to think. Then the vandal boys busted up her pots and tore up the flowers. It was such a shame. It really upset her. She could hardly keep them looking nice, and they'd get all busted up again. Seemed like her house was the only one targeted, too. Funny. Haven't had any problems with anything like that since then."

"Oh?" the man said, raising an eyebrow.

"Must have been some nasty boys from another neighborhood coming over to do mischief. Honestly. Some people. But not to worry, we're a real quiet neighborhood now. Anyway, sad... I do miss Peggy, she was a nice lady. They really weren't here that long. When they moved in, I got the impression that they were wanting to put some roots down, but then there was the accident, and he didn't stay after that."

"Did that real estate lady tell you about the staircase? So beautiful, but you'll probably want to do something about that first thing. It doesn't look that steep, but the steps are kind of short, and it could really do with a rail on the wall in addition to the banister. When they found Peggy, they said she must have flown right down, poor thing, cracked her head and broke her neck. Fell with force, they said. Awful. Do you have children? You won't want them running down those stairs, no sir."

"Well, actually—" the man said.

"Well, I see you have the moving van – such a blessing, movers. Moving is such a pain, and they are able to whisk everything in so fast. But you've already moved some things in, haven't you? I thought I heard some noises over there the other evening, and the lights were on downstairs. It was real late, but I thought I heard a thudding sound like something heavy getting moved around. I didn't see a vehicle, and I thought that was queer, but you must have pulled it around back?"

The man frowned, "Uh, actually —"

"Well, it'll be such a relief to get all settled. Do you have a lot of furniture? It's such a spacious house, I'm sure you'll find a place for everything. The attic is really big too, if you need storage. Probably needs a thorough airing out. Don't think it's been used since the Lattimers were here, and that was, oh, my, almost ten years ago. The house was vacant for a long time before the Johnsons. I think Mr. Lattimer used the attic as a private study. Queer, really, it's so cramped up there with the low ceiling and there are so many other rooms he might have used. No telling *what* he spent all his time doing up there. But the light was on in that tiny little window late into the night when the rest of the house would go dark. He was a mean-spirited old man. Never did like him."

She waved the trowel. "Anyway, Mrs. Johnson didn't use the attic, you know, she swore she heard heavy footsteps up there at night, but of course that's silly, there couldn't be anyone up there. I used to decorate for the holidays you know, and I always kept all that stuff in my attic. Too much trouble now, of course, I just put up a wreath and some electric candle lights in the windows. But you'll have plenty of storage space. It'll be so cheery to see that house decorated — oh dear, you *will* decorate for Christmas? A house likes attention you know."

The man frowned, "Yes, I suppose —"

"Well, I didn't mean to keep you. I'm sure you are quite busy, and I've got to get these flowers in. Anyway, it was very nice to meet you and I do hope you'll be happy here. I enjoyed our little chat and I look forward to meeting your family and talking some more. I'm sure we'll be good neighbors. You know, for a moment the other night when you were here, well… of course it was you, but for just a moment, I had the horrible feeling I saw the silhouette of Mr. Lattimer in your living room. Gave me a right good chill it did, I must say. Anyway, I'm so glad the house will be occupied again. That house has *so* much character."

Mrs. Peabody returned to humming and planting her annuals, the bun jiggling as she worked the dirt. The young man walked slowly back up his new driveway, looking up at the old house and back at the moving van.

Note

I lived in Japan for three years back in the nineties and was fascinated by the ghost stories. I will confess to being an estate sale and antique store junky drawn to old objects with character. The notion of tsukumogami, objects old enough to attain souls, intrigues me.

Ghost Light

I had been dozing for a few years, barely noting the changes in seasons, the comings and goings of customers and other objects in the shop. It wasn't likely that I was going anywhere. I enjoyed my spot on the high shelf close to the window with a good view of the store at a safe distance from those horrid porcelain dolls.

People are so contradictory, they always have been. Back when I was young, four hundred-odd years ago in Japan, people were more openly sensitive to spirits, frightened by noises that may or may not have been the wind. They believed in ghosts and *tsuku-mogami*, ordinary objects that earned a soul if they survived beyond the hundredth birthday.

Nowadays, distracted by electronic toys and gadgets, they ignore the rustlings in the curtains, the sudden, cool draft in the room. They want new machine-made furniture, the latest technology. Only a select few are drawn to the old things with soul and character.

As far as I know, the Japanese still tell stories of *karakasa*, haunted umbrellas or *moringi-no-kama*, haunted tea kettles, but now they laugh as they tell them. No one really believes the stories and no wonder, really. Who would keep a one-eyed, voyeuristic umbrella with feet? No doubt they were subdued and destroyed, probably by fire. But when I was young, I heard the story of a ghost umbrella that was lost in a monsoon. Later, it appeared all tattered and mangled and flapped around a village like a damaged sea bird, dripping water on market day shoppers as a harbinger of a rancorous storm. Afraid, they packed up hastily and ran for higher ground.

They did not laugh then.

And so few objects live long enough to take on a soul. Those that do usually end up like me, stuck in a dusty antique shop. At times, it's unsettling to be confined with all these energies, like that weepy escritoire over there oozing the essence of a woman dying of a broken heart. Or that shifty bookshelf against the wall that once supported the twisted library of a sadistic surgeon. The Oriental rug on the way to the bathroom hides maroon-brown bloodstains in the pattern, or does it? No one has bought it though the price has been marked down. People touch it and move away. Same with those "beautiful" quilts that tucked in the tubercular children and the cancerous old man…or that huge, rusty, cast iron skillet once used by a slave to cook endless tear-flavored cornbread. The smallest pan, the one on top of the stack, once brained an intruder. Who would want to eat morning eggs cooked in a pan with that energy—a mix of fear, guilt and vindication? There's that yellowed wedding dress, painstakingly adorned with pearls and lace…you'd have thought it would have sold ages ago. But it wasn't just nuptial jitters, you know. The bride should have listened to her fears. Oh, and then there are those sad stuffed animals on the four-poster bed whose children loved them to the brink of death, then grew up and discarded them.

How do I know all this? Trust me: at night, this place is noisy with psychic chatter.

I don't think my energy is negative. I've had a good life so far.

At the time of my hundredth birthday, I was living at the corner of the porch in a remote shrine in the Hokkaido mountains with Kanaka-san, the *guji*, or senior Shinto priest (in age and rank). He did not notice any change in me, though what I felt was indescribable. In humans it would be a cross between the adrenaline jolt of just getting down to business in the outhouse and seeing a snake, and awakening from an extended coma: a shattering clarity, a keen awareness. After a hundred years of dullness, I felt that I should have been bouncing around, making so much noise that the birds would spook from the trees and Kanaka-san would fall down in wonder. But none of that happened. That evening he shuffled around as usual, lighting us all (I was the last lantern on the long porch and the biggest, his favorite.)

He came to me, tried to light me with light stick.

I spluttered.

"*Aoandon*,[1] you need more oil, do you?" He harrumphed.

Kanaka-san's body put so much effort into basic functions like breathing, digesting and walking, that any extra tasks compounded the mental and physical strain. I felt badly that I couldn't help him. He left me in the darkening twilight, and carried a younger lantern with him to fetch the rapeseed oil jug. His shuffling and intermittent coughing receded.

A board creaked.

An owl called, *hoo-hoo-HOO!*

The air stirred as something passed.

I should explain that I did not sprout eyes like the umbrellas when I turned one hundred. Lacking eyes, I can only sense energies. As I have aged, the sense has grown stronger. It doesn't matter to me if I am lit or not, my blue light only helps humans to see what I feel.

Something smaller joined the first energy.

Kanaka-san's slippers swished closer, but stopped again as he leaned against the wall and worked through another wracking cough. He moved to the rail and spat, startling a mouse that ran

---

1 a Japanese lantern, or ghost light

down the porch rail to the ground.

"Let's see who we have with us, shall we, *Aoandon*?" Kana-ka-san said while pouring oil into my empty chamber. There would be no surprises that night, just the usual crowd.

He struck the light stick and touched it to me.

"Ahh. There we are," he said, blowing out the light stick and moving away to sit on a narrow bench.

It was always this way with Kanaka-san. Knowing he did not have much time left, he spent his days caring for the shrine and his nights making peace with his ghosts.

A thin, floral energy settled around him.

"It won't be long now, Michiko."

Not long after, Kanaka-san went to the well to fetch water and did not return. I felt the energies glide out to meet him and was happy that he would be reunited with the wife and children who left him decades before in a cholera epidemic. He had come to this shrine a grieving hermit. Now they could take him home.

Since the shrine had so few visitors and only intermittent cer-emonies to perform, the *gon-gūji*, associate chief priest often found excuses to be absent, leaving the *gon-negi*, junior priest in charge. Ryoto-san was a stout, clumsy young monk with brooding, dark energies. The energies would follow him, dissipating only when he was in the presence of others. Poor soul, he became so eager to greet visitors and chat with them, he earned the unfavorable nickname, *nure-ochiba*, or "wet leaf", as he was difficult to give the brushoff. He spent hours in prayers, slept poorly, talked to himself like a crazy beggar. The prayers and incense only pushed the spir-its back to the edges of the shrine where they huddled and festered.

The saké donations were Ryoto-san's undoing.

He began to drink to sooth his nerves, just a little at first.

"One has to honor a gift," he said, tossing back a shot.

The number of shots grew; the small glass was replaced with a larger one. The dark spirits followed the liquid spirits; they crept into his room at night and dug into his dreams.

One snowy winter night, he staggered out to the koi pond and drowned.

Time passed. I sat on a shelf.

I was two hundred and fifty, give or take, when I was bought at a street market by a jolly *okaasan*[2], Umeko. She and her husband, Takeshi were farmers with a house full of children, mostly boys. Their farmhouse maintained a busy, boisterous atmosphere of productivity and mirth. The few disruptive energies that stopped in out of curiosity were driven away again by their positive energies. Umeko had no need of my powers to reveal spirits, there were none to see. The children marveled at my blue light. After supper they told amusing stories and made shadow puppets on the wall.

That autumn, Takeshi's brother's family arrived to help harvest. The evenings echoed with mirthful laughter, enhanced with plum wine.

Takeshi's oldest son suggested that they all play *Hyakumonogatari Kaidankai*[3], that is, the telling of one hundred spooky stories. You'd think given that I'm a spirit lantern, I'd have known what this was, but at the time, I didn't. But I had a bad feeling about it all the same.

This "game" is fairly straightforward. After dark, one hundred thick candles are lit and a mirror is placed flat on a table. The participants take turns telling ghost stories, and after each story, the teller blows out a candle and looks in the mirror. Variations on this game, I learned later, involve three rooms. But this family only had the one room.

Obviously, it takes a while to tell one hundred stories. The children told nonsense stories they made up on the spot. The adults

---

2 *mother
3 one hundred supernatural stories

indulged them so they'd feel included. In a farming community, each person's contribution is essential to existence, and reinforced constantly.

Shadows grew in the room as the lighting diminished. I felt tentative gray energies coming, drawn to the stories. One of the younger boys, Minoru, was simple-minded, easily startled and confused. Not able to stay still, he rocked and moaned for self-comfort. I was sure he felt the energies too.

Takeshi's oldest boy began a story about a *bakemono*, a shape-shifting fox. His story was progressing at a disjointed pace when an insidious clawing sound by the window caught my attention. Although it seemed to be from a small animal, it was not an energetic signature that I was familiar with, certainly not an ordinary animal like a mouse or cat. The others were focusing on the story, looking forward at the table. They did not see the black shadow cross the floor. Minoru gasped as if unable to catch his breath. I suspect he saw the thing in my blue light.

I was sure Minoru felt the meanness of the thing as it scrabbled towards him, a large menacing energy in a rodent-sized body with delicate legs and grasping claws.

I wanted to get their attention and yell, "No, no, stop! Get more light!" But of course I had no way to do this. Or did I? I worked at making my flame behave in an erratic fashion, growing high and thin then waggling as if holding out against a stiff wind. A few of the younger children noticed.

The thing moved towards poor Minoru.

His mother patted him absently, "Hush now. Don't be rude. Listen to the story."

The thing hooked a paw on Minoru's exposed foot.

He flinched and screamed.

I channeled all my energy and tipped myself to the floor in a clatter of metal.

The girls screamed, Minoru flailed, several people jumped up and lit candles and lanterns. Soon the room had adequate light, Minoru's sister was cradling him in her arms. Minoru had pissed himself. Two of the younger girls cried and needed comforting. Their mother was distraught over their cries and embarrassed by the small puddle her son had made on the floor.

The game was over.

In all the confusion, I didn't know where that evil energy went. I hoped it left the house. I worried that it had attached to Minoru. It might have slithered into his ear or seeped into his heart. Would he have been strong enough to resist it?

The next day was busy with the harvest; the assembly were up before dawn and at it until dark. That evening everyone was too tired to socialize. They ate heartily but with little conversation. Afterwards, the dishes were washed, the children put to bed, the lights extinguished. No songs, no stories. I had only a glimpse of Minoru and thought he seemed more withdrawn than usual.

Takeshi's family left the following day.

Wisely, Umeko's family never suggested playing *Hyakumo-nogatari Kaidankai* again.

Two months ago, a middle-aged woman came in, wandered around and stopped in front of the weepy escritoire. She ran a hand across the top, stooped to look underneath, and walked around it a few more times.

The shopkeeper approached her.

"I can pull it out if you need a better look."

"My daughter wants to open a bed and breakfast. She's looking for a few antiques as accent pieces," the woman said, pulling a measuring tape out of her purse.

"Well, this one is in excellent condition. The drawers all open and close smoothly, and I think she'll love the elegant legs. It's very feminine but not fragile. It was built to last and was well kept."

The desk creaked in anticipation, so needy for love and attention.

Later that day, the desk was carried out and loaded into a small truck. With the departure of the weepy desk destined for a new home, a good old-fashioned torpor settled on me. (I'm old, okay? I can say torpor. It's a solid word.)

I tried to remember the last time my lamp had been illuminated. It had been when Melba, the psychic, died. Would I ever find a new home? In this day and age, who'd want a rapeseed oil lamp? I'd heard there was some newfangled something called solar lighting that was popular. More and more candle holders have come into the shop. Honestly, I never thought *candles* would go out of fashion. This frightened me. Candles are less fuss than lanterns, especially ones that use rapeseed oil.

And no one even knew about my special power.

"Don't get all glum" a concrete lion by the door advised. "Asian stuff is popular. People love those clunky pagoda-looking lanterns. You're way cooler than those things are. You've got artisanship."

This was true. I was commissioned by a witch and crafted in brass by an expert metal worker.

Perhaps with the coming of the short days of winter, I'd get picked up. *Kuso!*[4] Not long ago, an old woman almost bought that frightening black-eyed doll that could give a dead man the heebee-jeebees.

So how did I come to be in an antique shop in San Francisco?

I had passed from owner to owner, yard to shelf to barn for some time before being bought by an American tourist and shipped to Phoenix, Arizona. I was gifted to a psychic woman, Melba Frank. Everything and everyone liked her. Stray animals found their way to her. Birds peered in her windows and followed her around the yard. She was surrounded in a glowing, peach-feeling aura. She was an artist as well as a medium; her home was filled with large

---

4 Japanese for shit

canvases in bright collages of color. She set me by her front door on the edge of a rock garden.

It took her a while to figure out my talent. She came at me once with tiki oil, which would have been disastrous. Her hand hovered and then as if she felt every psychic fiber of my metal cringe, she backed away. "No, no, you are too old for this aren't you?"

Rapeseed, rapeseed, rapeseed.

"Perhaps I should do some research," she said and walked away.

She did. I would have done a cartwheel for her when she came back the next evening with a glass bottle of rapeseed oil. She poured. *Arama!*[5] How long had it been? She lit a match and touched me.

"Oh my." She stood back. "You are so beautiful." She sat next to me looking from me to the night sky. I loved these moments, sharing auras. Soon there was a white wisp, then an orb. The orb circled me and floated up into a tree.

The wisp gained form.

"Jenny?" Melba asked. "Your name is Jenny? How can I help you?"

Thus began a routine that lasted for years. Evenings outside with Melba and her spirit guests who came to communicate to the living, came for help, came for comfort. Many confused old spirits came from battlefields with gaping wounds and missing limbs. She guided them gently to the next world. Friends and family Melba had lost came to visit. Children came to find their parents, parents came to find their kids. And pets who'd been too confused to go into the white light. She guided them too.

When Melba died, she willed me to her best friend, Sarah. I'm not sure how we would have gotten along. Alas, Sarah had victim-energy. She was mugged one night and spent some time in intensive care. Her friends "helped" her by "cleaning" her house

---

5 Oh God!

and "getting rid" of the clutter.

Melba did one smart thing when she willed me to Sarah. She wrote a note and stuck it on my base. "Use with rapeseed oil only."

Over the years, I've learned how to attract or repel receptive people who are curious about me. This has been extremely handy, if you'll excuse the pun, since some scary people have handled me and considered adopting me over the decades.

Three weeks ago, a man of about forty picked me up. He smelled familiar. Yeah, yeah, I don't have a nose, but the smell is like a signature thing. Like you just know that cigar smoke, baby powder and the smell of wisteria are all distinctly different weights, values, signatures, even if you can't detect the smell. You feel it. This man felt like old Kanaka. *Just* like him.

"Use with rapeseed oil only, eh?" he read, righting me again. He spoke with an Irish accent.

It's me, it's me it's me. Remember. It's me. You know me. We worked together.

He had a non-sensitive friend with him. "What do you want that old thing for?"

"I dunno. It reminds me of something. Something from a long time ago. Maybe my grandfather's house."

No, older. From the shrine.

"Where the hell do you find rapeseed oil, anyway?" the friend asked.

"Oh, I'm sure it's still around. Gourmet shop or other…"

"It's just a lantern."

"It has character." He whispered, "I think it's *really* old. Look at the metal. That's Japanese writing, isn't it? I think it's worth more than the asking price."

His friend chuffed. "Whatever, man, you're the psychic."

Yes, yes, yes yes yes take me take me take me take me…

"I think I'll take it," he said, tucking me close.

"But, dude, you live in Ireland. Are you really going to lug it around in your suitcase?"

"I'm not *carrying* it to Ireland, though am I? I'm going on an airplane, silly."

Liam, is his name. This time. Liam lives in an ancient stone house on a cliff by the sea. I learned that in this lifetime, he has an international reputation and travels to do psychic work, which was why he was in California.

He set me on a flat stone a few feet from his front door. During the day the air is gray, moist, salty and filled with the sounds of seabirds. I have noticed an unfamiliar energetic pattern going on around the house. Small and benign, almost human, but no larger than a weasel and far more intelligent. And weasels are pretty smart. Liam seems to be aware of them, and sometimes addresses them.

He has had outbursts like, "Oh come on, then! Where've ye taken me book?" or "I left some cookies on the table for ye, now leave me be."

The little beings are less active at night. Like Japan, the Irish night hums with the echoes of ghosts, recent and ancient. Cries of women dying in childbirth; hoof beats of armies; drowning wails from ghostly shipwrecks, floundering swimmers, and a few lost souls who jumped off the cliff to meet the sea, not knowing they were fated to repeat that moment for eternity. Old phonographs could hold a stack of records then play them one by one. Here the ghostly recordings all play at the same time, some faint, some clear.

Unlike the mountain temple in Japan, tucked into the trees, this place is laid bare with no barrier from horizon to horizon — not a tree or hedge, only hills and stone. The sky is so breathtakingly vast, I'm glad to be near the house for reference.

I sat for three nights before Liam came outside with a dram of whisky and his dog, Berit. He crouched to protect the match flame against the night breeze. My blue light filled the doorway and part of his drive.

"Well, Berit, look at that."

I put all my effort into glowing the biggest brightest blue light ever.

We sat.

The dog sniffed the air, put her head back and howled low.

"Berit? What's got into you, girl?"

I heard a return howl on the wind. Faint at first, it came in waves sounding like a sustained screechy scream, half wailing woman and half hawk.

"That can't be good, can it, Berit?" Liam asked.

Berit backed closer to Liam and growled into the darkness.

The sound of a car engine and crunching gravel got louder. Headlights swung around as the vehicle came to a stop before us. The lights went out, a woman stepped out. I guessed she was in her forties. She took a few steps and stopped again, her voice tentative.

"Mr. Campbell? It's me, Gemma, Donal's daughter. I tried to call ye but couldna get a signal."

"You'd think I'd have reception out here, but I don't."

Gemma walked into my blue light. She had an honest, troubled aura covered with a layer of dread.

"I'm sorry to trouble you, but it's me Da. He's bad. They said you'd know what to do. Could you come ri' away? It's not fah."

Berit stood up and sniffed Gemma who patted her on the head. Although Berit found it comforting, I was sure, her fur was still raised.

"What's the problem?" Liam asked.

"You'll think I'm starkers, but I'm afraid. Terrified, really."

"Come. Sit here. Tell me."

Gemma sat on the bench by the door, hugging her coat tightly.

"Me Da's been livin' alone since Mum died. I know he's been lonely. I made a point to come 'round to visit and all, and he does still have his friends at the Old Goat in the village. For about a month, now, he's been avoiding me. Cancelling lunch dates and beggin' off from me comin' ta visit. I happened into the Goat and Owen, his best mate, asked me how I was getting along with his new woman! He hadna said nothing to me about seein' no woman. And tha' were kinda odd; not the kinda thing he'd keep from me. So I went round to check on him." She broke into tears and took a moment to gain her composure again.

"I went round to his house and let myself in. What a shock I had! I found him layin' about like he were half dead, not shaved and he'd lost a stone or more. The house was a right fright, too, not fit for pigs. Convinced he was sick, I tried to get him to tell me his symptoms. Oh! Gives me the chills it does! Expectin' him to say he's been ill, has cancer, or can't eat, has a fever, anything like that, no, he looks panicked and tells me to leave! I can't be there when SHE comes!"

She sobbed again. "I tried to...I tried to get him to shower...but he barked at me." She pulled out a tissue and blew her nose.

"There, there. Take it steady." Liam said, putting an arm around her.

"I went to put the kettle on, get him some tea and hunt up a biscuit. There were nothin' in the house! He hadn't been eatin'!"

She blew again.

"But he wouldn't let me touch him, wouldn't let me...he *cursed* me and sent me away! I've not given 'im no cause for this abuse. It ain't like 'im."

Gemma fell against Liam and sobbed.

"Has anyone seen the woman?" Liam asked.

"Well, I went back later with some groceries, after dark. At first, I thought maybe he invented the woman, maybe she was a delirium, but no. I parked down the road and walked up. There were only his truck ta the house, but as I got closer to the window, I heard voices. He were definitely talkin' with a woman."

Gemma gulped.

"I crept close and peered in the window. Everything *felt* wrong. Bad. For starters, there were no lights on, and that gave me the creepy-crawlies. It were supper time, and not even a kitchen light on. Then laughter and moaning. Me Da cried out and I almost rushed in, but I realized…it was revolting…they were having sex! Don't get me wrong, I'm not square or like tha'. If Da had a lady friend and were happy, honest, I'd be so happy.

But this was'na normal. There were animal grunts and moans, cries like agony from him. The sounds coming from that woman… she…she sounded like a demon! Her voice was'na natural, and I heard Latin and Gaelic in the growlin'." She sobbed again.

Liam stood up. "I've heard enough. We don't have much time. You suspect this has been going on for how long? A month?"

"Near as, yes."

"Do you have a safe place to go in town? Where you can be with friends?"

"Yes."

"Good. Give me a phone number where I can reach you. I'll call you when I have news. I need to prepare, but I will go to your father's house. I'm afraid your father has fallen victim to a *Leanan Sídh*,[6] an evil fairy seductress who is sucking the life out of him." He took Gemma's shoulders and got almost eyeball to eyeball with

---

6 LAH-nun-SHEE

her. "Do not follow me, do you understand? She's *very* dangerous."

Gemma nodded and stood.

Liam hugged her. "I'll do everything I can. Promise."

Gemma had not even left the driveway when Liam began bustling about. I heard him moving around inside, slamming doors, talking to himself. He reappeared with a duffel bag and a backpack which he loaded into his truck. Berit jumped into the front seat.

"You're coming too." Liam said, blowing out my light and carrying me to the truck. He set me on the floor of the passenger seat and cushioned me with a bit of blanket.

The roads in this region of Ireland prohibit one from driving at any speed without bouncing and banging about. Liam drove as fast as he could. When we arrived in town, Liam slowed and turned his lights off. We coasted towards a dark cottage at the end of a narrow road. Liam got out and Berit jumped out after him keeping close. Liam grabbed the bags and me and crept towards the front door.

The house felt dead cold and filled with a hungry darkness. I have felt all forms of evil before, and this insatiable, hungry-ghost energy is one of the most intense. Like a monsoon wind or high magnitude earthquake, it sucks you in, sucks you down.

Liam set me down. He fumbled with the matches and touched me with the flame. He laid a hand on top of me and whispered, "Help me see the truth." I knew what he wanted. Though he was a strong force, he needed to be stronger than the seductress in the house. If she directed her full power on him, he could be sucked in too. He needed my light to reveal her true form.

I focused all my energy of glowing at full strength.

Gemma had not exaggerated. The sounds coming from the dark house were not human. The man's cries were as if his fingers and toes were being ripped off one by one. The woman's voice changed rapidly from a snarling demon, a chanting man, a wailing woman and a screeching seabird.

Liam set down and unpacked both bags. He slung the backpack open and wrong way round, so his hands would be free and he could reach in from the front. He opened jars of salt and holy water and set them snugly inside the bag along with a handful of iron spikes. He tossed salt and holy water around the door frame chanting softly.

He picked me up by my handle. "Here we go."

He opened the door.

So occupied was the creature that she did not notice our entrance. The house smelled like death and rotten cabbage and looked about the same. It had clearly been a time since anyone had lifted a finger to wipe, dust or sweep. Like the aftermath of a vermin cotillion, the floor was littered with soiled laundry and broken pottery while fireplace ash footprints were evidence of mice and rats living large.

Liam flung salt as he walked. The course crystals made *sha-ta-tac-tac* sounds like light hail pellets as they cascaded down the walls and across the floor. He took a big swig of holy water and spat it as well. He took another big swig and held it as we walked toward the bedroom and the horrid noise. Berit took a wary position by the kitchen, her nose clearly overloaded with rank odors.

Liam eased open the bedroom door and set me down. The sound of the match strike was lost in the feral noises emanating from the small chamber. My light radiated into the room to reveal a skeletal man tied to the bed and a voluptuous red-haired woman rocking on top of him, her tail swishing side to side, pulling away to gather force and strike his flesh like a scorpion.

The man howled.

And these things happened in rapid succession:

Liam spat the holy water over the red-haired creature's head.

The she-beast turned. No doubt Donal had seen her as a beautiful woman, but with my light, her true form was visible: reptilian scales, lizard tongue, goat eyes that blinked sideways.

She hissed and shrank forward, away from Liam, undulating towards Donal.

Liam grabbed a handful of salt in one hand and threw it at her, showering her back.

She screamed and sprang off the twisted man, pushing off with furry goat feet.

Liam grabbed the iron spikes and lunged, planting one between her shoulder blades as she flew upwards.

She screamed.

Donal's eyes filled with the vision of her flying upwards, his mouth falling open. He collapsed back into the bed, so weak I thought he died.

I focused my energy harder than ever, turned my glow into a tracking beam so Liam could follow the creature. Liam flung another handful of salt and bellowed protection prayers. The creature flew toward the living room, Liam followed, taking a swig of holy water. She turned around and charged him, screaming. He spewed holy water right into her mouth, then ducked before she bit his face.

She gasped, tumbled, and flew toward the front door, but recoiled abruptly upon sensing the protection on the door frame. She banked off the wall toward the kitchen before spying Berit, now barking wildly, hair all raised on her back. The *leanan sidh's* tail swished as she shifted upward, hitting the ceiling.

Berit ducked; the scorpion whip just missed her shoulder.

The enraged entity clawed air towards the fireplace. I followed her with my light.

Liam raised more iron spikes and reached her just as she paused to go up the chimney. He drove two more spikes into her, one in the low back and one deep in her leg. With a last howl, she turned from solid form to vapor and disappeared up the chimney.

It was a long night.

Liam called Gemma, who arrived a time later with two friends and bags of fresh groceries. She bathed Donal, while the friends worked in the kitchen. One cleaned and sorted the larder while the other prepared a lamb stew.

When Donal was clean and dressed, Gemma fed him some of the stew with a hearty bread. All the while he murmured apologies to her saying, "I'm so sorry, my daughter. That was'na me. She had me bewitched. I thought she were so beautiful...such white skin and such fantastic eyes. Am I mad? Did she... really have a tail? Really have those devil eyes? Those hideous feet?"

"There, there, Da, it's all right now. Shh-shh."

"But did she really have a *tail*?"

"Shh-shh."

The friends swept and mopped the house, took out the trash. Liam worked his way around the house, smudging and marking it to clear out all the negative energy, block any further bad energies and seal it with protections. He marked the fireplace, every doorway and window as well as the major furniture, particularly Donal's bed.

As Donal slept, the others sat around the kitchen table finishing off the stew with beer in peace and silence. Words were too difficult, I guessed.

Later, as Liam blew out my light, he patted me. "I think we've done this before, haven't we?"

Yes, yes, yes.

Tonight, as I sit here with Berit and we watch Liam with his dram of whisky looking at the moon and listening to the night voices, I am exhausted, but happy. It will take me some time to recover my strength, but I should be fine if I can rest.

Liam is not a smoker this time, and not much of a drinker by Irish standards. Not bothered by age yet, nor a wracking cough, he is hale and hearty as they used to say. He and Berit often walk half a day or more together.

Gemma has been around to thank him and I'm not sure, but she has a signature similar to Michiko. Liam seemed to perk up when her car came in the drive again.

Liam is chanting a prayer to the night. And while I can sense distant funereal bagpipes, I also hear ghost children running and laughing…or is that the "wee men" as he called them, coming out to play a trick on Berit? She hates it when they pull her tail.

Note

I don't want to give away too much, but there are a few grains of truth to this story. I did go to Chattacon in the mid-eighties and I did see "it" at the end of the hall, as described.

And it freaked me right out.

Betty Hanson, Please Call the Front Desk

It's 1986, and a group of eccentrics and extroverts are converging at Chattacon, the science fiction convention in Chattanooga, Tennessee. I'm a senior in college. One spot left in the car for me if I want it. Not really a sci-fi guy, but sure, what the hell. I'd love to meet Lou Ferrigno.

A one-hour road trip crammed in the monster station wagon with a bunch of folks I don't really know, except my bud, Matt. The car smells like reefer and socks. Trees and rolling hills yield to the sprawl of Chattaboogie, then we're pulling in to the hotel. This is it! The lobby is packed half and half with awestruck newbies like me, and jaded regulars in extreme costumes. A Creature From the Black Lagoon bumps into me and a nerdy voice from within the mask says, "Sorry." Wouldn't think the real Creature would apologize for anything. We pile into the elevator with a Grim Reaper in a cheap costume, plastic harvester, knock-off black robe, blackened face barely covering pimples. He says nothing, tries to keeps in character, but he's just not convincing. A fat version of Gene Simmons with a remarkably detailed costume down to the platform serpent boots presses against the wall to let us in. His gut hangs over the huge satanic-looking belt buckle.

"This is so awesome!" a pixie-like member of our tribe coos, her Manga style, oversized blue eyes surveying the costumes. She giggles. She's kind of annoying that way. She giggles about anything. I keep forgetting her name. It's something like Deborah or Donna that doesn't fit at all. I think of her as Pixie-girl.

The doors open. Our sixth-floor room is in the middle of the long hallway. Matt had us roll gamer dice for beds, rollaway or floor. I get rollaway. Cool beans.

As we are stashing our bags in the room, an announcement comes over the hallway speaker, *"Betty Hanson, Betty Hanson, please meet your party at the registration desk on the first floor."*

"What are you going to do first?" Pixie-girl asks. She's actually bouncing.

Matt is studying the schedule. "Orson Scott Card is on a panel in an hour. I wanna see him. He's awesome."

Pixie-girl frowns. "I want to go to the sales floor and see what's for sale."

We ignore her. She leaves.

"What about you, Rod?" Matt asks.

I look over the schedule. "There's a Star Wars symposium. That could be cool. I might go to that." I've never been to one of these things before, I really don't know what to do. I figure I'll just wander.

"Yeah. Might catch that after OSC," he says and strides out the door.

I make sure I have the schedule, my wallet, a room key. I hit the john then head out. As I'm closing the door, I feel an intense menace, someone watching me. I nonchalantly glance over my shoulder down the hall. At the end of the hall is another Grim Reaper, in shadow, like there's an overhead bulb that blew out. This one looks real. He's sitting on a metal folding chair holding his sickle, right, but it's real. I can see the sheen on the blade. And he's totally still, staring down the hall. Alone. Waiting. How had we not noticed him when we came in?

I get a cold shudder through my body, like I stepped into the freezer at the pizza joint I worked at over the summer. *Why is he just sitting there?*

I look away. Closing the door, I scoot to the elevator. It's still at the eleventh floor. Great, not even close. I wait. I don't want to look down the hall again, but I can't help it, I do. He's so still, and I can't see his face at all. It really looks like there's nothing in the cowl, just darkness. I don't want to stare, I don't even want to look, but why can't I see any face? It looks hollow.

"Betty Hanson, Betty Hanson, please call the front desk."

The elevator dings. I squeeze in between two Storm Troopers and get a spot next to Judy Jetson. Her head is twice normal size and made of papier-mâché. Her skirt is stiff and pokes my leg. We get to level one and I follow the Storm Troopers to a small ballroom. Is that really Carrie Fisher? Sure looks like her. There's a huge Darth Vader too. Wow. Great costume, maybe it's the real one. I'm about to find a seat when a guard stops me and asks for my ID badge. Shit. I pat my pockets and realize I left it on the rollaway.

"Be right back." I trot out of the ballroom back to the elevator.

"Betty Hanson, Betty Hanson, please call the front desk."

Nuts. I wasn't paying attention. The elevator went down instead of up. The door opened to a basement ballroom. Jesus, is there a fire? No, just smoke. The hardcore, cigarette-dragging Dungeons and Dragons people tensed around tables with their sweaty, pasty-white skin— 'cause they never go outside except to scurry between buildings —glowing in the haze. Yelling. Dice rolling. My throat can't handle the smoke. I cough. Thankfully, the door closes.

Back up to the main level and a dude with a wildly curly blonde wig and a red spandex outfit steps in. Like a grown-up in Underoos. He looks pathetic. I realize he is trying to look like the Greatest American Hero. Poor geek. Some non-costume people like me get in too. The door closes.

Not Even Close to a Hero turns to me, eyes bright. "Isn't this so awesome? I heard Cassandra Peterson is a surprise guest. Can you believe it? Elvira? Here?" Little spittle-spots form in the corner of Not Even Close's mouth as he talks.

Sad puppy.

"Really?" I say real cool. I don't want him to latch on to me but I can't bring myself to be mean to him either.

When the door opens at level six, my floor, I'm thinking of getting away from him. I shoot out of the elevator. Immediately, I get that walk-in freezer effect again. I look to the end of the hall. Grim hasn't moved. The blackness around his costume seems to be seeping farther down the corridor. The whole end of the hallway seems like a gateway to a black hole. That is one helluva realistic costume, and *why the hell is he just sitting there?*

I got my ID and went back to the event. I had a pretty good time, actually. Better than I thought. It really was Carrie Fisher and I got her autograph! I saw Elvira, but she was mobbed with fans. I'll tell you this though, she is one bodacious babe, even though she's almost like my mom's age. Those are the real deal! And I shook hands with Lou Ferrigno, the Hulk himself. That guy is really huge. My hand disappeared in his, and I'm not a small guy. I bought a couple of comics, a dagger like from Dragonslayer, a VHS of Ladyhawke—Michelle Pfeiffer is *such* a total babe. I went back up to the room to drop it off.

This time, I'm in the elevator with some short ninjas and a Japanese girl dressed all in Hello Kitty. What's *that* about? I don't get it. I get off the elevator, there are two suits, a hotel manager and an assistant hovering around a door at the end of the hall. Someone is talking on a walkie-talkie. It's a cop. Grim and the chair are gone. Then I see a gurney getting wheeled out. There's a body on the gurney, covered with a sheet. The cop is now talking with a pudgy, slightly balding man who looks distraught.

"Mr. Hanson. You said you last saw your wife in the hotel restaurant...tell me, did she have any health issues, or had she complained of feeling poorly?"

I notice too, that I can see the end of the hall clearly again. No dim lighting. No freezer feeling. A normal hallway. I get a really bad chill anyway.

"No, nothing like that," he sobs. "She seemed perfectly normal. She was going to do a little shopping, we were going to meet up afterwards... You know...her family does have a history of heart disease. Her mother had a heart attack when she was thirty-nine..."

I'll just say this. I was at that convention all weekend. Ultimately, I saw three different versions of the Grim Reaper in the lobby, in the elevator, at events. But none of them looked like the entity I saw at the end of the hall. I asked around casually, and no one else claimed to see a hyper-realistic Grim either. Matt, Pixie-girl and the others hadn't seen or felt anything down the hall.

I want to say it was just a weird dude in a costume and maybe he was just waiting for a girlfriend or something. But, why just sit in the hallway? Why not wait in a room or downstairs? What about the darkness and that cold air? Did I imagine all that?

Note

The Dead Zone on Orlando's I-4 does exist, but the particulars of this story are 100% fiction.

Second Date

You never know what will draw you to someone, especially on a first date, and I never dreamed it would be a ghost. My first date, Rob, was human all right, but when it came to what we had in common, it was music, haute cuisine and Kenji Watanabe, who was seven years dead when we met.

My much hipper and more outgoing sister, Betsy nagged me into trying online dating.

"What have you got to lose?" she asked me.

"My mind."

I relented and spent a couple hours a week looking at my "matches." Most men sounded like egomaniacal monsters who wanted a perky, brainless twenty-something in disguise as a thirty to forty something. I was in my fifties and set in my ways. I wasn't about to coddle anyone. Rob's self-promotion caught my eye, however. "Love to read, garden, road trip to offbeat places, enjoy gourmet food."

We met for dinner at the Colombia House restaurant in Ybor City, Florida. He was on time, well-dressed and groomed. He approached me with military posture, smiled, and made good eye contact. Straight white teeth. I mentally checked some boxes in the pro column.

"You must be Vivian. I'm Robert Wright. Have you been here before? The roast pork promises to be phenomenal."

"I haven't, but I'm looking forward to it. I was relieved that your bio said you're an omnivore. Seems like nowadays its vegan-this, lactose that, allergic to nuts, can't tolerate gluten..." I waved a hand. Way to go sister, you're babbling already.

He smiled. "Nope. I'm good with all of it." Good indeed. Another check.

We were chatting away, enjoying roast pork "A La Cubana" and a red, Don Cesar Crianza as the employment questions rolled around. Rob related that he'd been a motorcycle cop for years and had a regular rotation on a stretch of I-4 near Orlando called the Dead Zone.

"That was rough. I don't miss that at all."

"I'm sorry, the Dead Zone?" I asked, feeling a chill creep across my shoulders.

"Yeah. Some people think it's just an urban legend, but trust me, there's something very creepy about I-4 near the bridge. I saw more accident scenes in that stretch than I care to remember." Rob wiped his mouth and pushed back from the table, his body language pushing back from the memory I thought.

My mind went back to a foggy day in Orlando years ago. I took another sip of wine, debating if I should relate the anecdote or let it go. Nervous, I plunged ahead.

"You know, a strange thing happened to me several years ago. I was on I-4 driving a rental car with a floaty accelerator. My old car made noise and offered more resistance as you accelerated, but this one could just fly. I wasn't aware that I was speeding, but I must've been. It was mid-morning, and the rush hour traffic was done. I was toodling right along, the road was clear. *Woop-woop-*

woop! I looked in my rear-view mirror, and there was a motorcycle cop right behind me. I'm pretty good about paying attention to the road. It seemed he came out of nowhere. I pulled over and pushed the window button down."

"Was it me? Oh, this is awkward, huh?" Rob asked.

"No, I'm quite sure it wasn't you. This officer was shorter, smaller, and had wide Asian cheekbones. He was wearing his helmet and sunglasses, so I didn't see a lot of his face...and, you'll think I'm nuts, but...there was something unnatural about him...I saw him park his bike, and then, before I even had my hand on my wallet, he was by my window. I remember I started. I suddenly felt very cold and uncomfortable. I mean, I know when you get stopped, you feel uncomfortable, but this was different. He hovered close to my door. I didn't want to see his eyes for some reason. I was really glad that he was wearing his sunglasses."

Rob's face paled, his mouth slackened. Uh-oh. Was I screwing the moment up? This date had been so promising so far.

His voice sounded wooden as he asked, "What did he do?"

"Well, that was kind of weird too...he didn't say *anything*. He pointed a gloved finger at me and I offered my driver's license. I was so nervous, I dropped it on the floor board and fumbled to get it. I could feel him so close, it was as if he were *in* the car with me." I looked down at my arms and held them out.

"Look! I've got goosebumps!" I rubbed my arms with my hands.

Rob swallowed.

"I know how edgy cops can be at a stop, but again, he didn't say anything. I passed him my card. He took it, scribbled a ticket and passed it to me. I took the ticket and my card and as I turned to put them on the passenger seat, said, 'thank you, officer. I'm so sorry. I'm not used to this car.' When I looked back, he wasn't at my window. I looked behind me and the bike was gone. I hadn't heard him start the engine or seen him drive away. I don't see how he could move that fast."

"So, what happened to the ticket?" Rob asked.

"That's the funny thing! When I got back home, my wallet and driver's license were on the passenger seat, but the ticket wasn't. I checked the floor, the space between the seats but it was gone. I didn't want to get a fine for not paying the ticket, so I called the police department and explained that I must have lost it, could they give me the reference number, and I'd send in a check."

"And they told you not to worry about it." Rob said with a slight nod.

"Yes! How did you know?"

Rob took a sip of his wine, swallowed, and set his glass back down. "I'm not sure you want to hear this, but that was a former partner of mine, Kenji Watanabe. He was a great guy and a great cop. Dedicated. Honest. He told me once that he came from a Samurai family, where honor and duty were everything. I trusted him with my life."

The chill bumps were rising on my arms again. I hugged my arms to my body and rubbed them slowly.

"Ken was on duty one morning like you described…the morning fog hadn't burned off as usual, there were still pockets on I-4 where all of a sudden you were lost in a cloud. Ken was first on the scene of a two-car accident. He pulled over to the side of the road and was on the horn for backup when a semi-trailer truck swerved, jackknifed and skidded. It struck him so hard that he and the bike were catapulted into the woods. More cars crashed and swerved into the tractor trailer. Bam! The view from the helicopter later made me sick, such a mangled mess. The rescue people didn't even know about Ken, there were so many cars and bodies to deal with. I guess it was fortunate for Ken that they said he probably died on impact, broken neck."

Rob eyes were watering. He paused and ran a hand over his short hair.

I covered my mouth with my hands. "I'm so sorry. I had no idea. I—"

"No, no, it's okay…I just haven't thought of it in a while. You know, it could have been me. I should have been on the beat that day, but he covered for me. My kid was having difficulty at school, and I took the morning off to go see his teacher and the principal."

"How long ago did this happen?" I asked.

"Seven years ago, in May," he answered.

"But, then…then it couldn't have been Ken who stopped me. I'm sure that I got stopped just a couple years ago, maybe three."

Rob glanced down at the table, then back up. Our eyes met.

"That's the thing, Vivian… it was Ken. I don't really know much about ghosts, heck, I didn't believe in ghosts until this happened. Several people have told the same story you told me. They were stopped for a traffic violation by a silent motorcycle cop. They got a ticket, but when they tried to find it later, it had disappeared. The few honest people called the police station. There was nothing logged in to the police records relating to their infractions. If they called, they were told not to worry about it, it was their lucky day. If they happened to send in a check, we put the money in a slush fund for office incidentals, to send flowers to the hospital for a downed officer. That kind of thing."

"Is that why it's called The Dead Zone? Because of the pileup that day?" I asked.

"No. There is a story that the highway was put in right over an old graveyard where a town of folks were buried. They had died from yellow fever. The cemetery was supposed to be moved in the sixties, but one day the DOT showed up with bulldozers then asphalt. The bodies were never moved. They are still under there."

"That's not very nice," I said.

"There have been an abnormal number of accidents on that road. More than any other stretch of road in Florida. To add to the weirdness, there are reports of people hearing strange noises coming over the radio…right in the middle of the song or news report they hear bits of moans, cries, warnings, or just static. Once they are beyond that bit of road, all is normal. I'm telling you, weird crap happens there all the time: cars break down, tires go flat, radiators blow up, drivers have heart attacks — all in that mile and a half of road. Believe it or not, some people have reported seeing orbs of light floating at dusk over the road, while others have seen ghostly forms clustered in the median, like a family huddled together for a photo.

I shuddered. I felt very sad for Ken who didn't seem to know he was dead.

"Are you saying that Ken is still out there doing his job on certain foggy days?" I asked.

"It seems that way, yes."

"Seems sad, like his spirit should be led to rest."

"Yeah. It does, doesn't it? I wouldn't have a clue how, though."

I smiled. "I think I can help."

My best friend, Annie was a professional psychic medium. When I related the story of Ken Watanabe to her, she was eager to help, and to meet my new date.

Rob and I kept tabs on the weather, and not long after our first meeting at the Colombia House, we met Annie on a foggy morning on that stretch of I-4 in the Dead Zone. We stayed well off the highway, near the woods. Annie closed her eyes and invited Ken to join us. She explained that we were there to help him. She complimented his years of service and loyalty to the police department but informed him that he had crossed over abruptly and needed to move on to the light. Rob held my hand as we listened to Annie talking in a confident and soothing voice. Like being at the beach, I felt the ions in the fog surrounding us in a slow chilly swirl.

"I see him…he's there." Annie said pointing a few yards away.

"Hello, Officer."

We looked where she pointed and saw a man in uniform standing next to a police issue Harley-Davidson Road King. In a dreamlike, Tai Chi slow movement, he held up a gloved hand and waved. Annie encouraged him to let go of his attachments and step into the white light. His form became less distinct and soon he and the bike faded into the fog.

Rob cried softly, which made us cry too. The three of us stood in a hug for a long time.

Annie was my maid of honor. Rob and I have been happily married for two years now. We enjoy travelling in our RV and are always on the lookout for a great restaurant. We avoid I-4 in Orlando.

Note

*The seed for this one was a writing prompt that asked for a
sensory trigger, a haunting sound or smell.*

Penny for Your Thoughts

John had been sitting in the waiting room for about fifteen minutes, his left leg bouncing up and down like a sewing machine needle. He fought with himself. A woman who had been sitting nearby glared at him and moved to the other side of the room with her magazine.

"He'll think I'm crazy," he thought. "I can't tell him the truth. I should go. This won't work." Yet he stayed. What other choice did he have?

Finally, the receptionist called, "Mr. Tatum? Mr. Barclay will see you now."

He was led into the office of Dennis Barclay, P. I. Mr. Barclay was a large middle-aged man with a wide fleshy face and a friend-ly smile.

"So, Mr. Tatum. How can we help you?" he asked.

He was not able to speak. He knew he must look crazy just sitting there staring. He should have taken another anxiety pill before he came, he thought. Where to begin?

"Mr. Tatum?"

John drew in a breath and gushed, "You have to solve a murder. An old one. A cold case. You have to. I can't go on."

Mr. Barclay who had expected a cheating wife scenario and a week of surveillance was taken completely by surprise. He looked skeptical.

"She won't leave me alone. And now--" He stopped abruptly and took a deep breath, then asked for a glass of water. Mr. Barclay got him a glass of water, and after several sips, he began again rapidly.

"The neighborhood I grew up in had small houses all close together. Kind of run down, but not bad. My house was next door to the Wilson's house. Penny was this little girl, a year or so younger than me. Her house had an old metal swing set in the back, close to the side of my house where my bedroom was. There weren't a lot of other kids on our street, and she had a swing set and a sand box, so I would go over to Penny's house and we'd swing or play in the sandbox."

"She was okay for a girl, you know. She was freckly, cute, and wore her hair in a ponytail mostly. She was sort of plain but nice, most of the time. She was emotionally troubled though, prone to serious meltdowns and temper storms. Sometimes we could hear her wailing and her mother trying to calm her down. When she got angry her face would get all twisted up and red. It was scary. Really intense."

Mr. Barclay tapped a finger on his desk. "Mr. Barclay, I hardly see where—"

John waved him off. "Now she would probably have been medicated, but back then parents just tried to cope, you know? She and I got along great though. She let me bring my trucks over. We would get wood crates to hold the sand that we'd wet with a hose and then flip over. We'd make them into buildings, and then I'd put in roads and fly my helicopter over the sandbox city. She liked to build really tall buildings, and she had little plastic people she put around the city." He was talking very fast. A spittle ball was growing at the corner of his mouth.

Mr. Barclay glanced at his watch. "Go on," he gestured, wheeling his hands.

"The swing. It was one of those old metal things that never seemed to anchor right, so when you got to swinging really hard, you could feel it trying to pop up out of the ground, you know? She loved the swing. Sometimes I'd be in my room, and I'd hear her next door, calling to me, "swing with me Johnnie, swing with me." So, I'd go over for a while. Sometimes I'd push her, and sometimes we'd swing side by side. I could always go higher than she could, and it would make the whole swing set bounce out of the ground. We would laugh."

"But that sound... always that sound. When you swung forward it wouldn't do it, it was always on the back swing, a high pitched, hiccupy squeak: *e-week...e-week...e-week.* Every day after school, I could hear her over there. *E-week....e-week...e-week.*" John stopped. He was staring at the carpet. His left leg was stitching again.

"Mr. Tatum? You said something about a murder?" Mr. Barclay prompted.

"It was the middle of summer — between first and second grade. She was starting school, going into first grade. She went missing. Her mother was hysterical, and my mother went over to sit with Mrs. Wilson. The police were everywhere. Then two days later, they found her body in the woods not far away. She'd been raped and killed. Oh, they didn't tell me about the rape part then, they just told me she'd been hurt and killed, but it was all over the papers and I figured it out much later. We were a small town. Most people didn't lock their doors. Crime to us was speeding tickets and shoplifting. The murder rocked the town. Things were never quite the same after that. The worst part was they never found out who did it. So, there was always the suspicion, the fear, and --"

"Mr. Tatum, are you asking me to solve a murder that is what, twenty – thirty years old? Surely if the police weren't able to --"

"You *have* to solve it, Mr. Barclay. You have to. I can't go on. The police won't help and she --" he stopped again and drank more water.

John began again, his voice more controlled. "Mr. Barclay... the night of the funeral, I was in my bed, trying to sleep. There was just a little moonlight coming through my window. I was thinking about Penny lying in the woods and about who could have done such a thing, when I heard it. *E-week...e-week...e-week...e-week...e-week.* For a second, I forgot – you know? I jumped up to look out the window, thinking that it was all a mistake and she was okay, and she was out there. It was night, she should have been in bed. It didn't make sense. But of course, it wasn't a mistake. Out the window in the moon glow, I saw the swing. It was moving back and forth like a steady breeze was blowing it. But you see, there was no breeze, no other branches were moving. And that sound kept going. *E-week...e-week...e-week.* I ran back to my bed and pulled the pillow over my head, but it wouldn't drown it out. Finally, I grabbed my pillow and a blanket, and ran into my parents' room. I slept on the floor. When they found me the next morning and asked why I was there, I knew I couldn't tell them. I said I didn't remember. They assumed I'd been sleep walking."

"Every night I heard the same thing: *e-week...e-week...e-week.* Then, sometimes I could hear her calling, "Johnnie. Come swing with me. John -- nie, come swing with me." Once I was so sure she was there I looked out the window, and she *was* right there, on the swing. She was a filmy blue, but quite distinct. I could see her ponytail, her clothes, her shoes, her face. But where her eyes should have been, there were just empty black holes. She was raising her hand and waving me to come over. Those empty eye sockets, Mr. Barclay, I almost pissed myself when she turned her head and I saw those black eyes."

Mr. Barclay leaned back and frowned.

John continued, "I never said anything to the Wilsons or anyone about it. I think the Wilsons must have heard the swing sometimes too, or maybe they couldn't stand the reminder that she was gone. Either way, one day it was gone. I was so relieved! I thought that would be the end of it. Oh, no. That night lying in bed, almost asleep for once and then of course it came: *e-week...e-week...e-week* and her voice, "Johnnie. Come swing with me. John — nie, come swing with me!" She'd get more and more insistent. I learned to sneak into my parents' room and sleep on the floor and get up before they woke up and go back to my room."

"I thanked God when my dad got transferred, so we had to move away. New town. New neighbors. I thought it was finally over. I'd be free, right? She appeared in my dreams. Beckoning. Waving me over with the ghost hands and those empty eyes and always calling, 'Johnnie, come swing with me.'"

John Tatum licked the spittle ball from his lip. His eyes darted like a cornered animal. "Of course, I avoided playgrounds--they were right out, I'd almost always see the swings moving, and I'd know she was there."

Mr. Barclay leaned forward and folded his hands. "Mr. Tatum. You are telling me a ghost story. You understand that I can't possibly solve a murder that the police couldn't solve based on a ghost story."

"Oh, but you have to, Mr. Barclay. You see, I've already been to mediums who have tried to contact her. They say she won't leave, go to the white light or whatever until her killer is found, only she won't even give any information. I don't think she knows who killed her, so it must have been a stranger. The psychic said that surely, she would be haunting the killer if she knew who it was, but she doesn't, so she's focusing on me. I've been to therapists. I've tried psychoanalysis. I've had prescriptions for anxiety and been told by some that I am delusional. I am not delusional, Mr. Barclay. I am haunted, and I am extremely desperate."

John was now leaning half way across Mr. Barclay's desk as if ready to pounce. He backed off a bit and continued, a new spittle ball forming at the corner of his mouth.

"In the beginning, I tried to talk to my wife about it, but it has put such a strain on our relationship, and if I don't get help, she could divorce me and I'd lose her, Josh, everything. I can't have that. I don't know how to solve the murder and Penny won't let me be. She's gotten so much stronger, oh so much stronger. In the beginning it was just the sound. Then I could see her. Filmy. Ghostly. But now -- she's been waiting so long, and she's been getting so much stronger. And she's so angry. She wants attention. She wants her murderer caught. I don't know how to help her, and she won't leave me alone. You simply have to help me. You see, just yesterday, I picked my son, Josh up from daycare. Do you know what he told me? He told me that when they played outside, he met a nice girl – guess where? Oh yeah, on the swings. He said she had her hair in a ponytail. She was sweet, kind of plain, but nice. Do you know what she said to him? "Swing with me, Josh. Swing with me."

That evening, on his drive home, Mr. Barclay reviewed Mr. Tatum's story in his mind. Crackpot. Impossible. Ridiculous. Ghosts. If the man didn't leave him alone, he'd get a restraining order. He couldn't wait to tell his wife, Missy what an odd day he'd had. Such a nutter. It was Friday too. He was looking forward to a nice relaxing weekend. Maybe he'd go fishing.

When he pulled his Honda into the driveway, his wife and daughter were in the side yard. They had obviously been talking over the fence with the woman next door who was heading back to her house. Missy smiled and waved as she approached his car. Anne skipped towards him. Beyond Anne, he noticed the top of a new metal swing set in the neighbor's yard.

"Welcome home, honey," his wife said cheerily. "We were just meeting the new neighbors, they just moved in today. They seem very nice. The Winthrops. Betty Winthrop is a librarian and she likes to garden. Mr. Winthrop will be the new branch manager at the City Bank. They have a little girl Anne's age. She seems very nice. They just finished putting in a swing set for her. That'll be so nice, Anne'll have someone to play with. The girl's name is Penny, isn't that right, Anne?"

Missy Barclay noticed that her husband's face suddenly looked a bit ashen. "Honey, what's wrong? You look like you've seen a ghost."

Mr. Barclay stared at the metal peak in the neighbor's yard.

"It's nothing, dear." He patted her hand but felt distinctly queasy.

Over dinner that night, he decided not to mention his visit from John Tatum. Mrs. Barclay thought that her husband seemed oddly moody and reticent. She decided not to prod. He'd tell her when he was good and ready.

That night, Mr. Barclay was spooning with his wife. Her breath was slow and steady, and she was snoring, just a little sigh on the outbreaths. In breath, pause, *prrrr*. In breath, pause, *prrrr*. It was very comforting. Mr. Barclay wished he could fall asleep. There was a bit of moonlight coming through the sheers. What was that sound? Another rhythm. A kind of a squeak. At first, he thought it was his imagination, but it got louder. There could be no doubt. *E-week…e-week…e-week…e-week*. Mr. Barclay looked at the clock: 12:30 AM. *E-week…e-week…e-week*. It went on and on. 3:30 AM. *E-week…e-week…e-week…*

What had Mr. Tatum said again? "You have to solve it Mr. Barclay, you *have* to. She's been waiting so long and has been getting so much stronger."

3:45 AM. He heard the voice, very faint and child-like coming from outside, "Dennis. Denn -- is. Come swing with me. Dennis! Come swing with me!"

He could see now that he would have to solve the murder. He just had to.

Note

I wrote two versions of this story. Feedback was split 50/50 when I asked people which one they preferred. Both have strengths; I can't decide either. Since it's so short, I offer the two for you to decide.

No Corny Monster Story
(Palatka Version)

Do I believe in Bigfoot, Sasquatch, or the Florida Skunk Ape? You bet your ass. No question. I grew up in Palatka, Florida, which to a passerby is not much. Single story shops, nothing to get excited about. A half decent fish house, a quaint downtown historic district. Otherwise, it's auto body, beauty-aid and thrift shops. Palatka is a pit stop between the potato capital of the state and a generous swath of pine forest. I was a senior at Palatka High School (Go Panthers!) I talked my girlfriend, Mary Anne into going to Robinson's Farm for the haunted corn maze. It was a local place that had a fruit stand out by the road, and fields in the back near the woods. They had the cheesy fair games, a haunted shack, a haunted hay ride and a corn maze.

Mary Anne didn't want to go, and I should have listened, but my best friend Tony and his girlfriend, Viv were going. I wanted to go. We talked her into it. We started with the haunted shack, and you know, it was all dark and creepy, and monsters and freaks would pop out at you, then they locked you in a room, you couldn't get the door open, a group of ghouls would surround you and paw at you. Pretty good make-up actually. Poor Mary Anne was the closest to the door screaming and pounding to get out --

she bruised her hands pretty badly with the pounding. After locking us in, of course they opened the door super-fast, and we all fell out like Mo, Larry, and Curly, which was kind of funny. The door slammed shut behind us. Viv jumped and squealed. Tony and I laughed.

Mary Anne was all freaked out and said she wanted to leave. We called her a chicken and wandered through some of the silly carnival stuff, you know, spin the witch, win a prize. We all got some drinks and fair food; she got a hot pretzel, I got a corn dog. Viv got a giant blue cotton candy as big as her head. We wandered some more. Mary Anne calmed down.

We talked her into the haunted hay ride. We told her she'd be safe, nothing would mess with her in the middle of the wagon. Kids were going on it, right? She relented. We were sitting on the bales of hay going really slowly in the dark. It seemed really lame. Just the sound of the tractor pulling us through the darkness. All of a sudden, there was a burst of fog and moaning zombies came out of a graveyard and chased us, some of them climbed on the wagon--one of them grabbed someone and pulled him off the wagon screaming. We figured the guy was a plant, you know, to make us think he was one of us.

We rode through a trailer park—serious trailer trash junk in the dirt yards, the trailers un-level, grungy, falling apart. Some hot babes came running out half-naked with leather collars and ropes around their wrists like they'd been locked up. They screamed for help and ran toward the wagon. Just as they got close to us, some redneck thugs in overalls emerged from the woods firing guns. They rounded them all up and dragged them back towards a dilapidated shed. The chicks were still screaming and pleading, "Please save us!" as they disappeared from view.

There was a calm as we rode around some more. It was quiet. Again, just the sound of the tractor plodding along. Was that the end of the ride already? No. An enormous combine tractor blasted its lights on us. It was *right* behind the wagon, with all its machinery grinding and whirring--like any minute it would start chomping the back of the wagon — it seemed alive like an insect-faced Trans-former, a crazy-huge pissed-off farm truck. Mary Anne screamed a lot, but afterwards she said she thought that was fun. We got let off right near the corn maze.

Viv and Tony followed a group of teens into the maze; Mary Anne and I were behind them. She was pressed up tight against my side, holding my arm. After the first two turns, the lights behind us were lost. It was dark as shit. New moon. No flashlights allowed, just the glow sticks on the ground. That hemmed in feeling from the tall corn all around. It muffles sounds, you know? With all the turns, we got pretty disoriented, pretty quick.

Dudes all in black with glowing ghoul faces popped out of the corn right next to us. Mary Anne jumped and stumbled into me, mashing my foot. Her head bumped my jaw; I bit the inside of my lip hard. I put my arm around her and we moved forward.

Of course, the dudes with masks and mock chainsaws came out of nowhere and circled us. I heard Viv scream ahead of us. Mary Anne screamed too, pressing into my chest. The guy yelled something like "You're going to DIE" in a deep spooky voice right next to her head, she bugged like she was going to bolt. I grabbed her arm. She yanked on my arm so hard, I thought sure she'd dislocate my shoulder. She freaked and started whining, 'I want to get out! I can't do this, I'm too scared!' Up ahead, Viv was pretty freaked too. The chainsaw dudes disappeared back into the corn, and it was quiet again. Tony and I told the girls they could walk in the middle of us, so the spooks couldn't get them. We moved forward all arm in arm like in *The Wizard of Oz*.

We must have been at the back of the maze where the corn field was up against the pine forest. It seemed even darker, much darker, and quieter. We had gone a few turns with no spooks. Viv and Mary Anne were relaxing just a little. Suddenly, right next to us a raspy voice whispered 'kill, kill, kill, kill!' just like in the Friday 13th movies, and Jason appeared, you know, with the hockey mask. He grabbed Mary Anne's arm. I didn't think they were allowed to touch people. Mary Anne wigged out. She broke away screaming, 'I can't take it!' She grabbed Viv and they took off running. I feel so badly now, but we were laughing then. It was funny how bugged out they were. Tony and I weren't too worried, we figured we were almost to the end, we'd meet up, right? Shit, I can't help crying. I feel so guilty...we thought it was all fun, you know?

It was really dark back there. And spooky quiet. Then there was this smell. This rank, garbagy, putrid, skunky, noxious odor. It was heavy, just blanketing us. We stopped. Tony, gagging, asked, "What in the hell is that *smell*?" We heard some movement in the corn, and that's when I heard Mary Anne scream. Then Viv. They were just ahead of us somewhere around a bend. I heard Viv start screaming for Mary Anne, then for us, then just out-of-her-mind screaming, a harsh shriek turning into a high wail then like hysterical blubbering. I had a flashlight with me, so did Tony. We turned them on and ran towards the screaming, tripping on dried corn stalks.

We came around a turn and saw Viv on her knees screaming hysterically – her eye makeup streaked on her face—God, I can still hear that scream. She flailed an arm toward the corn to her right. A hulking, hairy man-ape thing – it was like ten feet tall with a huge hard, boney-looking head like a gorilla--growled at Viv like King Kong, and then picked up Mary Anne--she was--oh Jesus--she was limp and had blood on her arms and big c-claw marks. It carried her off into the corn. The teeth--so big--and that stench. We were so shocked.

For a second, I thought it was like the dude on the wagon, you know? All a joke, and he'd bring Mary Anne right back. But that smell lingered, and that was no spook costume. That thing was real. Those teeth were real. The deep claw marks on Mary Anne's white arms... She was so limp like a half-bag of laundry. She was so tiny, anyway, poor thing. I puked that corn dog right up until I had dry heaves.

The aftermath was awful. They only found her purse and one sneaker. The police insisted we were perpetrating a hoax. If I had been alone, they would have locked me up for sure. Thank God,

I had witnesses. The only ones who believed us were the wackos who wanted to interview us about our Skunk Ape encounter. And poor Viv. She was never the same after that. She became a recluse and got addicted to anti-depressants. Not that I've done much better. Most of the time my closest friends have names like Jack Daniels and Jim Beam.

I had to tell Mary Anne's parents what happened. God. I could tell they didn't believe me. Mary Anne's mother rushed at me pounding her fists in my chest, shrieking "what did you do with my girl?" Great boyfriend I turned out to be, too stunned to chase after it to try to rescue her. But if you'd seen it--if you'd--God, it was *huge*. Tony and I talked about it afterward and agreed that we probably couldn't have stopped it. Maybe if we had followed it instead of running for help, we could have saved her, but I don't think so. It was there and then it was gone. It moved so fast. The cops said the corn was too trampled that it was impossible to tell even find a trail to follow. I don't think they looked too hard. They kept on asking me the same questions, trying to get me to change my story.

Turns out, Robinson's farm was smack dab in the middle of Florida Skunk Ape habitat—ha! ha! I didn't believe in that crap, I thought it was a stupid urban legend. But I saw that thing, and I smelled it—God, I will never forget that smell. That was no damn hoax. And poor Mary Anne's body was never found.

No Corny Monster Story
Alternate Version

On the Saturday night before Halloween a few years ago, my wife Jill and I had invited some friends over to hang out. We had watched the move *Halloween*, the first one, and had migrated outside to sit around our new fire pit. I had dug it out and made a concrete and stone wall around it. It turned out pretty awesome. We'd had some trees come down in a storm last year and had plenty of logs for a great fire.

We sat in deck chairs zoning out with the glow and the crackling, resting our feet on the wall. It was a crisp night with an almost full moon, and few clouds to interrupt that mystical glow where the twisty, water oak limbs and Spanish moss swaying slightly in the breeze are illuminated. Someone suggested taking turns telling ghost stories. I thought I could handle it.

I was on my second Heineken, when Lindsay finished her story about the New Jersey Devil, a creature known to haunt the southern Pine Barren region of New Jersey.

Ken was saying, "Oh that's crap, there's no such thing as Big Foot or the Jersey Devil."

I had been huddling close to the fire, not wanting to admit that I was cold.

"You can say what you want," I said, "but I saw one. They're real."

"Sure you did, Dave," Ken mocked.

"I did," I said. I took another swig of beer. "It was the week-end before Halloween. I was a senior in high school. I talked my girlfriend--" God, it was all coming back to me, the corn maze, the sounds of the fake chainsaws, the screaming-- "Mary Anne – I talked her into going to Dudley's Farm for the ghost walk and haunted corn maze. It was a local place that had a fruit stand out by the road, and fields in the back. They had a hay ride, a haunted shack and a corn maze." I took another big swig of beer. "She didn't want to go, but my best friend Tony, and his girlfriend Vivian were going, so we talked her into it." I felt jittery. I remembered the relentless interviews afterward, having to face her mother and tell her…

"We went through the haunted shack, and you know, mon-sters would pop out at you, then they locked you in a room, and you couldn't get the door open, a group of ghouls would surround you and paw at you…they did a pretty good job. Good makeup. Poor Mary Anne was the closest to the door. She was screaming and pounding on the door to get out, she bruised her hands pretty badly with the pounding. Of course, they opened the door really fast, and we all fell out like Mo, Larry, and Curly. Then the door slammed shut behind us. Tony and I were laughing, but Viv and Mary Anne were kind of shaken up."

"Oh no way!" Jill said. "Remind me to never let you talk me into a haunted house."

I would never. I downed the rest of the beer and got up to get another one out of the cooler. Jill threw me that look, but I pretended I didn't see it. Beer in hand, I sat back down and continued. I saw the carnival lights in my mind. Heard the screams from the haunted house again.

"Well, we wandered through some of the booths, old timey silly carnival stuff, spin the witch, win a prize -- she kind of calmed down. We did the haunted hay ride. We were sitting on the hay wagon on bales of hay, it would drive really slowly in the dark, nothing happening, until we passed a small graveyard and zombie lurched out and chased us. Some of them climbed on the wagon. One of them grabbed someone and pulled him off the wagon screaming. We figured he was a plant, you know, to make us think he was one of us. That was cool. Almost convincing. There was another calm as we rode around some more. It seemed kind of lame, just riding in the dark. Then, all of a sudden, an enormous combine blasted all of its lights on us. It was *right* behind the wagon, with all its machinery grinding and whirring – it would have started chomping on the back of the wagon— it seemed alive like an insect-faced Transformer, a crazy-huge pissed off farm truck. Mary Anne screamed a lot, but afterwards, she said it was fun. That was cool." I was breathing hard. I tipped up the beer bottle.

"Next we entered the corn maze. We weren't allowed to use flashlights. There were glow sticks on the ground -- that was it. It was dark as shit. New moon. That hemmed in feeling from the tall corn all around. It muffles sounds, you know? Like we could hear other people, but with all the turns, we got pretty disoriented, pretty quick. Of course, the dudes with masks and mock chainsaws came out of nowhere and circled us. Mary Anne was yanking on my arm so hard, I worried she would dislocate my shoulder. She was screaming like hell. Dudes all in black with glowing ghoul faces would pop out of the corn right next to us. Mary Anne freaked and started yelling, 'I want to get out! I can't do this, I'm too scared!' We told her she could walk in the middle of us, so the spooks couldn't get her. Her best friend, Viv, was pretty freaked too."

I looked around at everyone staring back at me. I swallowed hard. "By this time, we must have been at the back of the maze, where the corn field was up against a pine forest. It seemed darker, much darker, and quieter. We heard a raspy voice nearby saying 'kill, kill, kill, kill' just like in the Friday 13th movies, and Jason appeared, you know, with the hockey mask. Mary Anne bugged.

She broke away screaming, 'I can't take it!' She grabbed Viv and they took off running. We weren't too worried, we figured we were almost to the end, we'd meet up, right?" I felt a tear starting in my left eye.

"Dave, are you alright?" Jill asked. Oh, God, I'd never told her this before. I waved her hand away. I had to keep going.

"So, Tony and I were walking and talking you know, and we both noticed this smell. I'm talkin' rank, garbagy, putrid, skunky, noxious odor. It was heavy, just blanketing us. We stopped. We were gagging and thinking, 'what in the hell is that *smell*?' And that's when I heard Mary Anne scream. Then Viv. They were just ahead of us somewhere around a bend. I heard Viv start screaming for Mary Anne, then for us, then just out-of-her-mind screaming. I had a flashlight with me, so did Tony. We turned them on and ran towards the screaming, tripping on dried corn stalks. We came around a turn and saw Viv on her knees flailing and gesturing at the corn to her right. And then we saw it, this hulking hairy ape thing – it was like ten feet tall – it growled at Viv, - oh, Jesus-- those teeth!-- and then picked up Mary Anne and carried her into the corn." I was shaking badly and felt tears tracking down my face.

"It had teeth – so big--" I lost it.

"Oh my God," I heard Jill and the others murmur. Jill came over and hugged me hard.

"Jesus," Ken said.

I wiped my eyes and took a deep breath. My voice was all jittery when I spoke again. "The aftermath was awful. They only found her purse and one sneaker. The police insisted we were perpetrating a hoax. If I had been alone, they would have locked me up for sure. Thank God, I had witnesses. The only ones who believed us were the 'wackos' who wanted to interview us about our Skunk Ape encounter. And poor Viv. She was never the same after that. She became a recluse and got addicted to anti-depressants. Ha hah! I spent a long time with my best friends Jack Daniels and Jim Beam, too. Shit. Turns out, Dudley's farm was smack dab in the middle of Florida Skunk Ape habitat. Ha hah! I didn't believe in that crap, but I saw it, and I smelled it. And poor Mary Anne's body was never found."

Well, you can imagine how the evening went after that. Awkward! It was "oh look at the time" and "hey, we should be going" and then it was just Jill and me. I wanted to apologize to her that I'd never told her before, and I could tell she wanted to say something to me too, but somehow neither of us could find words. She cleaned the kitchen and went to bed. I sat staring at the fire, images from that night in the corn maze round and round in my head like mental chewing gum. It was very late when I finally went in to sleep.

We've been invited to Halloween parties since that night around the campfire. Bless Jill, she always comes up with a plausible excuse for why we aren't able to come. She knows I can't handle it.

Note

I don't recall why I had to pass through Port Authority as a young girl, alone, but I remember dim lighting, funky smells and stepping over homeless people to get to the bathroom. I was relieved in more ways than one to get out of there. I joked then about the likelihood of a hidden gate to hell.

Surfing the internet to see if things have changed, I found several other references to poor signage, grime and a sense that there may be a secret gate to hell.

This is purely fiction, but…you never know…

Final Call

Tonight is the fortieth anniversary of The Night I Will Never Forget. The day had been ordinary until class let out into the frigid night. Mother's dark blue Volvo station wagon was waiting outside my ballet class right on time, its exhaust and fogged windows a welcomed sign of promised warmth. I hurried to get in. The sun had just set; the temperature was destined for the twenties that night. I had pulled my jeans and sweater on over my leotard and tights, which helped a little, but my jacket and scarf were not holding up against the polar wind of Vermont in my twelfth year, October 1976.

I noticed my backpack and suitcase on the back seat as I buckled my seat belt. Mother didn't want to look me in the face, but I could see her eyes were puffy, watery and red.

"What's going on?" I asked. She clutched out and began driving. We turned left instead of right at the light.

"Your father," she began and swallowed hard. A tear dropped in her lap. She tried again, "I've called my sister, your Aunt Lucy, and she will meet you. You are going to go stay with her…you'll be safe. I think it's best for now. Just for a few days until…" Another tear fell. "I am putting you on a bus. I wish I had the money for a plane, but I just can't right now. There's a bag with some sandwiches and snacks. It'll be a long trip, but once you change buses in New York, you'll stay on the same bus. She will meet you at the bus station."

"But Aunt Lucy lives in North Carolina, doesn't she?" I asked, thinking that maybe somehow she was much closer, staying somewhere else, and I wasn't really going to be on a bus by myself from Vermont to North Carolina. At night. Alone. With strangers.

"Sweetheart, you'll be all right. Just be a good girl and pay attention. Sit up front near the driver so he can keep an eye on you." She pulled a wet tissue out of her sweat suit pocket and wiped her nose.

***

She had stayed with me until the bus came. We sat in the Volvo listening to the radio. It was October thirtieth. She found a station that played old timey shows running The Whistler. Kind of lame but kind of creepy in the dark at the bus station with the wind woo-woo-wooing out there and the street lamp shadows twitching with tree branches swaying.

She hugged me fiercely and kissed the top of my head. "It's just for a few days honey, until…"

I remember a time when my Dad was like a normal Dad and sat at the table and talked at dinner. Taught me to ride a bicycle. But something happened after his motorcycle accident. He hit his head, and it was like he died, and some imitation Dad took his place. He wasn't fun anymore. He yelled. Got violent. We moved out after he hit Mom a few times and spanked me with a belt. Mom said that we'd be fine after the divorce, but it seemed like she'd been saying that for a long time now. The new medication was supposed to help his mood swings, but I hadn't seen much change. I was afraid of him most of the time.

There weren't many people on the bus, thank goodness. I'd be able to push up the arm rest and almost get comfortable across two seats. I looked out the window at my mother trotting in place to stay warm, trying to smile. I spread my hand wide on the window. It was cold. Warm tears formed in my eyes and found slow pathways down to my chin. The bus pulled away. Mom held her jacket with one arm and waved vigorously with the other. My mouth developed uncontrollable tremors and my vision was blurred with tears.

Mom had said, "You'll have to get off the bus at Port Authority in New York City. Go directly to the lower level to gate sixty-eight. You'll get on the bus going to Nashville, Tennessee. Be sure to tell the driver you are getting off at Asheville, North Carolina. You should be there first thing in the morning. She'll take you to Shoney's for breakfast."

I had ridden on buses by myself for short trips, but nothing like this.

***

I woke up suddenly. Another stop, and someone was moving to the back of the bus coughing one of those painful, phlegmy, heaving smoker's coughs that make you cringe and suddenly grateful for your own health. The bus began moving again.

I had eaten a sandwich and some cookies earlier. There was a yucky taste in my mouth which made me want my toothbrush badly. I assumed Mother had packed it in my suitcase, but I didn't want to look for it. It was dark out. We were in the countryside somewhere. Trees and road. I fell asleep.

I woke up with a start to bright lights and groaning, grinding bus sounds as it struggled around tight turns in a huge terminal. There were quite a few people on the bus now and they seemed to all be gathering their bags in anticipation of disembarkation. I swung my legs down and looked out the window again. There were clusters of travelers bundled in dark winter coats and scarves huddled around oversized duffels and bags with handles and wheels. The lights came on in the bus and we were allowed to get out.

Port Authority smelled like piss, socks and diesel fuel. I gripped my backpack and suitcase so no one could snatch them from me. The gates around me were numbered in the four hundreds. I was nowhere near sixty-eight. A family of heavy people speaking Italian swarmed around me, bumping me, tripping over my suitcase. I felt invisible and terribly alone. I had to pee desperately.

Like a person trying to cross the street during the running of the bulls in Pamplona, I made my way purposefully through Port Authority following the little woman symbol for the bathroom. Arrow this way. Walk. Turn. Arrow this way. Finally, a small hallway and the glowing light of a restroom was in sight. To get to the door, I had to step past a mini village of homeless people. The rank smell was overpowering. I pressed my face into my scarf. This was it. I was going to be mugged and killed for my backpack and suitcase right here and now. I wanted to scream with how badly I had to pee and yet desperately did not want to move any closer to these scary sad people lying about by the door in waiting. I had to pee. I ran, hopscotching over extended legs. I shot into a vacant stall and swung the lock shut.

Now I was locked in. They would probably creep in after me and jump me when I opened the door. Worse, I was still wearing the leotard and tights! Crap! I'd have to get mostly undressed! I put the paper down all over the toilet, took off top clothes, yanked down the last layer, and tried to pee. I'd been holding it so long, it hurt, but I couldn't start. "Oh, please on please oh please let me pee and escape and live through this," I prayed.

"You'll be fine, just pay attention."

I relaxed enough to pee like a donkey. I finished and planned my escape. I pulled up the tights and leotard, shimmied back into my top and coat. I'd quietly open the door and whip it open and run so suddenly that they wouldn't have time to grab me. I unlocked, sprinted and hopscotched back out to the main hallway giddy with relief that they had not mobbed and mugged me in the bathroom.

I ducked around an elderly couple looking around clearly as lost and bewildered as I was and spotted a dark man in a drab uniform with ID badges on a lanyard around his neck.

"I'm trying to get to gate sixty-eight. I'm lost. Where would I find it?" I asked.

"Take the elevator over there to the Lower Level. Should be down there." He said.

I thanked him and ran to the elevator.

I was mashed into the elevator to what seemed like beyond the maximum capacity, my backpack against one wall digging into my back, and a red-haired woman's hot pink hard case digging into my shins. It seemed like the molecules in the air in Port Authority must be plumper and dirtier than anywhere I'd ever been. It was hard to breathe.

And then the door opened, and we exhaled out of the elevator. It was oddly warm on this floor. The fluorescent lights were fluttering, dead or dying; it was very dark gray and there was a strange caustic quality in the air above the other smells of piss and grime. An old man missing an arm and most of his teeth ambled past me, his tongue restless in his mouth. A woman's cackle, like a witch, sent a shiver down my spine, as a dwarf with a mangled foot hobbled quickly by me. He turned to glance at me, and he had one eye that was all white. Poor man! I'm sure I tried to seem unaffected, but he had given me the creeps and I'm sure I flinched.

To be clear, it was not the eye, the club foot or the dwarfism that made me flinch so much as the total package of suffering, physical and mental, that exuded from him as he hurried like a terrified woodland creature, not a man catching a bus.

The faded yellow sign for gate sixty was just across from me. I tightened my grip on my belongings and moved forward with purpose. "If you walk with purpose, you are less likely to be a victim." I had been advised once.

Sixty-two, sixty-three, sixty-four…That awful smell was getting stronger, and was it my imagination or were the people here getting creepier, or was this Homeless Central? A crazy man crabbed along next to me ranting about "Never know what I've done, I've been a naughty, naughty boy! Yee-hee!" I stopped so he would get ahead of me. It was definitely warm, I was sweating now. Even the floor felt warm through the soles of my sneakers.

Then I saw it.

You'll think that I was over tired, or emotionally distraught, a child with a wild imagination, but this is exactly what I saw. Where there should have been a bus gate, there was a narrow tunnel. A red glow illuminated the gate number and I could have sworn there were three sixes. The last one was very dim, but it was there. A tall man with a frightfully red face, like the most horrid sunburn, wearing a black tie and tails, although the 'tail' was red and longer than normal, stood at the entrance like a doorman or sentinel. Behind him, small red flame pot sconces hung along the walls leading to the back of the tunnel like in a set from cheesy Vincent Price movies of Edgar Allan Poe stories.

"Last call," he hawked like a seasoned carny. "Last call, step right up, time to go." His hands were terribly withered and wrinkled, both holding the top of a ball- handled cane. He looked up and down the hallway, then spotted me, with large, gold goat eyes. He smiled, and a long tongue slithered out below his chin, licked the air and snaked back up into his mouth.

I screamed and ran. When I got to gate sixty-eight, I looked back, panting. I blinked hard. For there with the red-faced man with the lizard tongue was a haggard man, his hair all wild, his clothes disheveled…and…he looked just like my father, the darkest, saddest version of my father I had ever seen.

I heard his voice, more in my head than down the hall, say, "Goodbye. I'm so sorry. Forgive me." The haggard broken Dad man lifted his arms in a slow shrug and blew a kiss to me! Then he and the red-faced man walked forward into the tunnel and the hallway was empty. There were no further deformed beings at all, it seemed they had all passed into the tunnel.

The bus driver asked, "Are you all right, little girl?"

"I just saw this horrible man with goat eyes…"

"Hmm. We see all kinds 'round here, 'specially on Devil's Night. Where you goin'?"

"Is this the bus to Nashville, Tennesee? I'm going to Asheville, North Carolina."

"It surely is, honey. Get in. We'll get you there like Cinderella to the ball."

The rest of the trip was fairly uneventful. I must have dozed off a few times, although the shock of seeing my father prevented me from relaxing or truly sleeping. My Aunt Lucy met me just like Mother said she would.

The following day, on Halloween, Mother called to say that my father had committed suicide the previous evening.

Mother moved to North Carolina to get a "fresh start."

I never told her what I saw on Devil's Night at Gate 66[6] at the Witching Hour.

Too upsetting.

Note

This story was published online in 2014, appearing in Volume One, Issue Two of Crooked Shift:

http://gentle-peak-9324.herokuapp.com/

A big thank you to Matt Rotman, Editor-in-Chief for picking it up.

This is offered up for the Nathaniel Hawthorne and Edgar Allen Poe readers who have patience for a Victorian-style, slow build of creepy. I know you are out there.

Find a Relic, Pick it Up
And All the Day You'll Have...

To be satisfied with a little, is the greatest wisdom;
and he that increaseth his riches, increaseth his cares;
but a contented mind is a hidden treasure,
and trouble findeth it not.

-- Akhenaton

Friday 21 October 1904

Dear Diary,

I regret the lapse of time since I last wrote; so much has happened in the last few weeks. I have attempted several times to set the pen to the page but was unable to begin to address all that has transpired. On the 12th of September, Mama and Papa were due back from a missionary trip to a small community in eastern Pennsylvania.

I had stayed behind to sit with my good friend, Miranda, who was recovering from a bicycling accident in Central Park. The poor thing was merrily sailing along and startled a flock of pigeons which flew all around and in her face. She lost control of the bicycle and careened into a rhododendron bush. While she did not break any bones, thank goodness, she suffered substantial bruising and a badly twisted wrist.

We awaited news of my parents' return but heard nothing. I had hoped that they had simply been detained and did not have time to send word, but then on the 14th of September we received the shocking news that they were both run down by a steam engine while crossing the train tracks at that deathtrap, Grand Central Terminal. After disembarking, and while attempting to cross the tracks, Mother's boot heel caught in a rail. Father tried to free her, but her foot was stuck fast, with not enough time to untie it and free her. Another passenger attempted to assist them, but he smartly jumped clear at the last second. The driver claimed he had not seen them until it was too late what with visibility so obscured by steam and soot.

I have such tumult in my heart that God would allow missionaries, doing his good work, to be struck down, not while out in some wild region, but here in modern New York City, while exiting the train station. Such loving kind souls forever lost to us. At times I am overwhelmed with grief and cannot bear it.

Uncle Ely has accepted me as his ward and I have come to live with Uncle Ely on Canal Street in the apartment above his curio shop, The Djinni's Trove. He has been away in Mexico, but his maid, Flossie, who is hardly older than I, has been very kind to get me settled and keep me company.

Pansy

Find a Relic, Pick it Up, And All the Day You'll Have...

Saturday, 22 October 1904

Dear Diary,

It is a perfect autumnal day today with the leaves approaching peak coloration. The air has that early morning crispness, and I should be in good spirits to be here in the heart of New York City, but alas my heart is heavy, and I lose myself in just staring out the window. My chamber window looks out onto Lispinard Street, which quieter than Canal, has delivery wagons passing regularly to the service entrance of the Brandeth House Hotel just beyond my view. Coming from my quiet neighborhood in Danbury, Connecticut, the commotion from the street is disquieting. Meanwhile, the house I was raised in, the only house I have ever known is to be sold. I am deracinated and overcome with despair. I wish I could say that I look forward to Uncle Ely's return, but I am apprehensive. I earnestly hope he does not resent my imposition into his household. I have never spent a significant amount of time in his company, the odd holiday gathering perhaps, and even then he considered me a child not worthy of more than passing attention. We are fundamentally acquaintances, practically strangers.

My chamber is small but very adequate, and the bed is quite comfortable for which I am grateful, even though I sleep fitfully. Flossie is an excellent maid of all maids, for while she is childlike in experience and deportment, she is very diligent at cleaning.

The front parlor is clearly that of a bachelor, with heavy chairs and a massive sofa with balled feet. This room appears as a natural extension of the curio shop downstairs. A tall display cabinet contains a collection of carved animals in jade, wood and soapstone. A wild boar snarls with great teeth exposed; an ox reposes peacefully, and a very delicate swan floats gracefully, gazing out into the room. One shelf contains all manner of short curved blades, daggers, stilettos and switchblades. Several Persian teapots sit on the mantel beneath the great mirror. Next to Uncle's chair there is an imposing ceramic black panther as tall as my waist sitting up like a sleek house cat expecting to be fed. By the window is an elaborately carved humidor.

I look forward to tomorrow when Mother's friend, Mrs. Cross has offered to come fetch me in the morning to join her for church at First Presbyterian on Fifth Avenue. She and mother were close friends and she misses her terribly as well. I am confident that she will understand my despondent tendencies and I shall not have to feign a cheeriness I am incapable of mustering. I'm very fond of Mrs. Cross; like the most desirable aunt, she is a very soft woman, kind and undemanding.

Pansy

Sunday, 23 October 1904

Dear Diary,

First Presbyterian is so majestic! We arrived well ahead of the service time, and a very good thing it was! Mrs. Cross said that often hundreds are turned away as so many wish to attend and cannot be accommodated. Such a different experience from our regular congregation in Danbury! The choir sounded truly angelic, as if a doorway had opened to heaven itself. After the service, Mrs. Cross took me round on a tour of the church and provided some history. It was completed less than thirty years ago. I am much moved to have been able to attend service today and very grateful for Mrs. Cross for including me. I prayed for Mama and Papa, and for Uncle Ely's safe return.

Pansy

Monday 24, October 1904

Dear Diary,

I woke this morning to the clamorous cawing of crows. When I rose and looked out the window, there were four large crows on a ledge above the shoe repair shop opposite – they were level with my window and all four were cawing as if directed at me. It was most unsettling.

I had hoped to get out for a walk in the park with Flossie today, but it seems that rain is imminent. The sky is growing darker.

Pansy

Tuesday 25 October 1904

Dear Diary,

Crows again! This time there were five, and as before, they obstinately cawed in my direction. I recall old legends that crows are harbingers of evil, and if they tap at your window, it means someone will die. Oh, I do wish they would go away!

Another peculiar incident took place after I had dressed and was about to go down for breakfast. I glanced out the window again to see that only one crow remained, and thankfully it was silent, although it stared in my direction which was disquieting. Then I discerned an eerie singing, faint at first, but it grew in volume. There were three young children in thin, shabby coats skipping around in slow circles on their way down the street. They were singing slightly out of tune and gesturing as they moved, sometimes putting hands on hips, sometimes hopping. Just as they reached my window the song reached a crescendo and they all collapsed to the ground in a heap and began laughing. One little girl glanced up and looked directly at me. She was not laughing or smiling. I waved to her hesitantly, but she did not respond. They got up, and began the song and swirling dance again, and soon disappeared around the hotel. Why had she looked directly at me? How had she known I was there? My nerves have been so unsound since coming here…

Pansy

Tuesday, 1 November 1904

Dear Diary,

Last night was All Hallows' Eve. Yesterday afternoon, Flossie and I went marketing and saw some school children dressed in costumes in the school yard. So endearing! There was a tiny waif dressed as Little Red Riding Hood, another was bedecked in a witch costume with a giant black hat, and a little boy was dressed as a pirate, another as a ghost. A few of the children struggled with their costumes as, unaccustomed to wearing them, they found the cumbersome apparel impeded their motion. For some the material sagged, for others the accessories confounded them -- hats fell over faces, the pirate sword tripped the pirate. One little boy, removed from the others as if rejected or feared by them, was clad as a beggar. His garments were oversized and gray with dark stains all around. His motions were not in the excited fashion of his fellow classmates, but in slow, measured steps, his feet dragging in the dirt. His gaze was fixed on the ground. Abruptly he paused, lifted a rock and smashed it down on the ground repeatedly. The suddenness and viciousness of this action distressed us both, and we removed ourselves.

A storm is expected for tomorrow. Great dark clouds began forming in the afternoon and a wind gained momentum during the evening. We have not heard from Uncle Ely regarding when he might return from his travels but Flossie wanted to dust the Trove today in the event that we were to get word of his pending arrival. She asked me to keep her company. It has been some time since I have been to visit Uncle Ely and I had forgotten the dark and mysterious nature of his curio shop. Upon entering from the street, one encounters a human-sized wooden ferret in the form of a witch doctor. Upon its head rests a skull headdress adorned with feathers and beads.

He holds a stout staff in his left hand, and a mystical talisman in his right. His face is wise and grave. The shop abounds with such unusual and often sinister objects -- statues and masks from Africa with piercing eyes and glowering countenances and dolls from Haiti that look utterly malevolent. There is a stuffed giraffe head on the far wall, its melancholy eyes gazing across the room in lament. How ever could someone kill such a gentle creature? Who would want a giraffe on their wall staring down at them? It is beyond my reckoning how Uncle Ely greets each new acquisition with excitement and elation.

Not all of the acquisitions are so gloomy or frightful. Uncle does have a fair number of antiques and ceramics that are rather elegant. There is a pair of Chinese vases of which I am quite fond. Under an elaborate lapis blue border are three ladies at a tea party with graceful cranes flying above them. There are also display cases with jewelry, watches and other accessories from various parts of the world.

The wind was unflagging. Before supper, Flossie and I struggled to re-secure a shutter that had liberated itself and had begun banging insistently. After supper, a damp chill settled over the apartment. Altogether with the shadows, the wind and the afternoon spent in the shop, I had no need of an All Hallows' Eve ghost story to agitate my imagination.

Pansy

Thursday 17, November 1904

Dear Diary,

Three crows this morning persistently cawing. Oddly, they only perch on that ledge opposite my window. This causes me such agitation that I find myself trying to wake earlier and earlier and get out of bed faster to escape the noise. Now sometimes I hear the cawing in my head even when they aren't there. I feel persecuted, which is preposterous, but there it is all the same. Flossie has seen them too, and believes they are wicked.

I have heard from Miranda who has recovered completely. We hope to go ice skating in Central Park this afternoon if it doesn't rain. Unfortunately, that seems very likely.   Pansy

Tuesday, 22 November 1904

Dear Diary,

I am to go stay with Violet and Raymond for the Thanksgiving holiday. Raymond will meet me tomorrow at the train station and we will travel together to New Haven. Flossie and I will lock up the house and secure The Djinni's Trove. Flossie will join her cousins in the city for the holiday weekend. It will be such a comfort to be with Violet, as I can imagine she mourns Mama and Papa as intensely as I do.

Pansy

Monday, 28 November 1904

Dear Diary,

Raymond and Violet have a cheery little house and they made every effort to make me feel welcome. They are such happy newlyweds and such a handsome couple with a bright glow about them. Thanksgiving was somber without Mama and Papa, but we had a lovely dinner of ham, pheasant with cranberries and rolls, and amused ourselves with word games. I joined them for church yesterday. Their church, as in Danbury, was small, intimate, and elegant in its simplicity. The weather was mild enough to go on an outing to East Rock and clear enough that we could see Long Island from the cliff top. I was very grateful for the company and the leisurely ramble.

I woke up with a start this morning, my heart wild. I had been dreaming that a raven was on my window ledge looking in at me. His eyes glowed yellow. When he opened his great beak, he unleashed a shockingly forceful shriek. I glanced outside and was enormously relieved that there were no birds of any kind to be seen!

We got a letter from Uncle Ely that he is passing through Texas and expects to be home by the weekend. I am glad and uneasy in equal measure.

Pansy

Friday, 9 December 1904

Dear Diary,

Uncle Ely has returned at long last and has settled home. He has opened the shop and asked if I would mind catching up on some cataloging of his inventory. We have spent several afternoons going over ways in which I might assist him in attending to customers or preparing items for shipping or delivery. He has been very patient and says that he is pleased at how I have taken to these tasks. Towards late afternoon, between the atmosphere of the shop and his steady pipe smoking, a mounting nausea develops such that by evening I readily retreat upstairs. Still, the activity does help to occupy my mind, and I am grateful for the companionship, though Uncle Ely is more contemplative than conversational.

Pansy

Sunday, 11 December 1904

Dear Diary,

I attended church with Mrs. Cross this morning. The choir was as angelic and uplifting as usual. Alas, the sensation of bliss and grace was fleeting. After church, Mrs. Cross asked if I minded awfully going on a drive to drop off a gift for a friend uptown. A fine rain was coming down, like a falling mist, almost imperceptible while the damp slithers into the bones. My hands and feet were cold, but naturally I said I would not mind at all. New York in winter is so very bleak. The bright leaves of autumn have all gone, and the bare limbs of the trees reach out despairingly.

We paused momentarily in front of the Brennan Mansion on 84th Street and Mrs. Cross mentioned that is was the home that Edgar Allen Poe had lived in for a year, and purportedly wrote "The Raven" while occupying it. Oh, if Mrs. Cross had any notion of how I have been plagued with crows at my window and the evil raven in my dream! Was it just a coincidence or something more sinister? I chided myself. Of course not. Her friend's home was just a few blocks down 84th – it was perfectly natural that we passed this landmark.

This winter has affected me most strangely. Ordinarily, fanciful imaginings do not occupy my mind, but I cannot seem to strain them out.

Pansy

Wednesday, 14 December 1904

Dear Diary,

I have been weak with congestion, headache and chills since our outing on Sunday, and have slept most of the days away in fitful episodes. I've had dreams of the raven again, and one last night of evil children carrying away a bundle like a newborn child. On several occasions I have had the eerie feeling that I am not alone in the room, but once fully awake, naturally there was no one else there.

Uncle Ely has been very kind and concerned about my health. My earlier fears that he would be cruel or resent me in his home were completely unfounded. I am weary but filled with gratitude for his goodness.

Pansy

Monday, 19 December 1904

Dear Diary,

I was not quite well enough for church today but assisted customers in the shop this afternoon. Sales have increased with Christmas coming. We've sold a Korean chest, some jewelry, and several Oriental bowls and vases.

I am so looking forward to Christmas!

Pansy

Thursday, 28 December 1904

Dear Diary,

The Christmas holiday was lovely! Uncle Ely and I went to visit with dear Violet and Raymond in New Haven. Their cozy little house was all festive and cheery with the delicate candles, bright paper and crocheted ornaments in the Christmas tree and the holly and pine boughs on the mantel. Raymond's parents and sister came for Christmas dinner. We had a lovely lamb with boiled potatoes and a pudding for dessert. After dinner, we played charades which was very jolly, and Violet played on her spinet. She has always been so accomplished; Raymond beamed with pride. She has said that he has been thoughtful and loving and I could see it in his eyes beholding her. Uncle Ely puffed away on his pipe contentedly. He did not join us in the charades, but the edges of his bushy moustache turned up with amusement, and he clapped encouragement. It was good to see him in good spirits as he is prone to a rather solitary existence. He does not have friends to speak of, nor does he go out to socialize at his club.

Violet announced that she is expecting her first baby late this spring! She suspected that she was with child before Thanksgiving but wanted to be sure before she shared the news. I look forward to being an aunt! I have started embroidering a receiving blanket for the baby. May God forgive me, I confess to feelings of jealousy towards my sister. She got beauty, grace and talent, while I received a frail body with plain features, and if I had talents bestowed upon me, they have yet to be discovered. All the same, I am delighted for Violet, she deserves every happiness and blessing.

Despite all the good cheer and exciting news of the coming baby, the absence of Mamma and Papa was felt very keenly. This was our first Christmas without them. We tried very hard to keep our grief at bay but did lapse into quiet moments of melancholy reflection.

Pansy

Sunday, 1 January 1905

Dear Diary,

Happy New Year! What a magical evening we had last night! Uncle Ely and I took the subway to what used to be known as Long Acre but, since the completion of the New York Times building, is now called Times Square. The Times building is grand but so isolated, tall and narrow, like the very last sliver of cake remaining on a cake plate. There was a festival with all manner of food, jewelry, and clothing vendors, along with jugglers and fortune tellers. Last year was the first year the fireworks were displayed at Times Square, but I had a wretched cough just after the holidays and none of us went out. I was positively determined to see it this year! Last evening was frightfully cold, but thank heaven, the sky was clear, the wind was calm and the fireworks were simply grand -- but so loud! The soot floated down like great, dark snowflakes, I even had some catch in my eyelids. The sound frightened some of the smaller children around us, but overall the atmosphere was wonderfully gay. There was such frivolity and hope in the air! It was so moving to be in such an enormous crowd, swept up in the sentiments of hope and celebration. They said over 200,000 people attended last year, and surely this year's number far exceeded that. Once the sun set, it would have been difficult to stretch an arm out straight, we were shoulder to shoulder all evening. Uncle Ely warned of pickpockets and offered to guard my beaded purse for me. I purchased some pretty New Year cards from one of the sellers and will occupy myself writing well wishings to mother's friends this evening, especially Mrs. Cross. She has been so kind to me taking me to church with her on Sundays.

Today is clear and cold. There are just a few snowdrifts remaining, and they are dark brown with street dirt. It was so splendid to get out last night. This winter has been hard, and dreary, and with the holidays passed, despite the promise of a new year, it is challenging to hold optimism when January stretches before us only to be followed by more of the same in February.

When we got back home, Uncle Ely surprised me with a gift.

A tiny kitten! He had been hiding her downstairs in his shop. She is a bit weak and has a wobbly back leg, poor darling. She was the runt of the litter. I have named her after my favorite children's book character, Katy, from the Carr novels by Susan Coolidge. Katy, like myself, suffered from illness and was bedridden but recovered and went on to have charming adventures. Kitten is so small and vulnerable, she reminds me of myself as a child. Perhaps I was a runt too. She is so small, she often curls up in my old slipper by the fire and fits within it completely.

Uncle Ely is not one for sentimentality, although on occasions, as with Katy, he surprises me. For all his gruffness, he means well I believe — he is forever speaking to me as if I were still a child, and I am now nineteen! He did not want to allow Flossie or myself to decorate for the holidays but conceded that we could put a wreath on the door and have candles in the front windows upstairs. He did not decorate his curio shop in the slightest. In fact, it remains a peculiar space caught in its own time, a dark place that seems to have more shadows than it ought, they seem to come right out and challenge the lights.

Flossie, whose Scottish mother bestowed upon her delicate child ears all manner of stories of fairies, witches, goblins, banshees and the like, now refuses to clean Uncle Ely's shop unless I am present. (I will not disclose this to Uncle Ely as he would likely be furious. It is our little secret.) Frankly, I am grateful for her company as I am ill at ease in the shop as well. Flossie has named the giraffe Bartholomew, and now sometimes we include Bartholomew in our conversation for a giggle. He's less ominous that way.

Uncle Ely remains an enigma to me. I sense at times that he harbors a great heartache or injury that he cloaks with his private countenance. He rarely speaks of himself or his past. Once I approached him as to whether he had ever been married. He laughed and said that "tangling with a woman would inevitably lead to a passel of children and weigh him down like a barnacle encrusted naval anchor." Yet, there seemed to be a disconsolateness about his face as he said this. I shall have to ask Violet if she remembers

Papa ever mentioned anything about Uncle Ely's past.

1905. A new year.

I pray that this year will be a tranquil and happy one. I hope to expand my social horizons and perhaps I too, like Violet, might find eventually find a loving and kind husband. In the meantime, I am filled with gratitude for the blessings I have, known and unknown.   Pansy

Saturday, 7 January 1905, First day of Epiphany

Dear Diary,

Mrs. Cross and her nephew, Wyatt came to fetch me for church last evening.   I had not seen Wyatt in quite some time. He is just a few years older than I and I must say, he is handsomer than I recall! He is in his second year of teaching science at Hotchkiss, the preparatory school for boys in Lakeville, Connecticut. On our ride up Fifth Avenue towards First Presbyterian we had a chance to re-acquaint ourselves. He expressed to me how sorry he was about the loss of my parents and asked how I was adjusting to living with Uncle Ely above the curio shop. I told him about New Year's Eve at Times Square and helping Uncle Ely at The Trove. He recounted some very amusing stories about the pranks the students had pulled on him as a new teacher last year.

I recalled that we had last seen each other two years prior at an All Hallows' Eve party. There had been word games, apple bobbing, and ghost story telling. He had told a story about how he had seen a ghost on the stairs in his house as a young child. It had given us all quite a fright. Mrs. Cross cleared her throat and pointedly shifted to discuss the evening's Epiphany service and how beautiful the church would be filled with candles representing coming out of the darkness into the light. She fixed her gaze on the pair of us and it was quite clear she was discomfited by the discussion of All Hallows' Eve. Indeed, I was looking forward to the night's service. As expected, it was lovely -- so much more intimate with the low lighting, groupings of candles all around and then each congregant holding a candle as well. Reverend and Mrs. Hargrove greeted us warmly afterwards and expressed how pleased they were to see Wyatt again.

On the ride back, we took up our conversation again, talking about all the new buildings going up in the city and the new subway stops. Wyatt asked me if I had ever been to Coney Island, I said no, but I had heard it was like a fairy land with all the electric lights at night. I have a post card on my dresser with a picture of the arcade. Mrs. Cross suggested that we should all have an outing to Coney Island when Wyatt returned for a visit at spring holiday.

"I promise we won't have to visit the House of Horrors." Wyatt teased.

It is raining this morning; the drops are aggressively pelting at the windows. I will help Flossie with the wash this afternoon, there is little else to do. As we are not expecting anyone tomorrow, we might as well start early. It will take so long to air dry it all.

Katy is batting at my ankles. It tickles! Even she is feeling restless today.

Pansy

Sunday, 8 January 1905

Dear Diary,

It is with a heaviness in my breast that I write on this dismal morning. The temperature plummeted during the night, and the rain turned to sleet then to snow which has not stopped since late last evening. An arctic wind gained strength and is now rattling the windows. The sky is as gray as my thoughts. Today marks the third anniversary of that dreadful New Haven line train wreck and once again the same grisly photographs of the wreckage have been in the newspapers at the news stands. Mamma and Papa have been most keenly in my thoughts. I miss them so! There have been several more victims of the trains since, yet the Vanderbilts ignore the outcry.

It is so frightfully dreary today, I feel like a caged canary. With the weather so horribly inclement, I did not expect Mrs. Cross and Wyatt to come to fetch me, and this has put me in a sour disposition. Wyatt will be going back to his work soon, and I am quite sorry to miss seeing him again today. I can look forward to more washing and wringing today.

I am not lacking in any regard and should not like to complain, but I do get lonely here. Without dear Flossie, I'm sure I would not know what I would do. It was lovely to get away to visit with Violet and her Raymond in Connecticut while Uncle Ely was off in Mexico, and again at Christmas. To be quite honest, the gloom of The Trove wears upon me.

Uncle Ely has had me helping him with cataloging his inventory and I have had to spend increasingly more time there since his return in November. I wish it did not have an access door to the main house and only had the street entrances. Just crossing over the threshold, I have the sensation of a shroud passing over my shoulders. I have examined what causes this unnerving sensation and have determined that it is precisely because the Trove contains nothing living. The great giraffe is dead; the African masks, the dolls all are lifeless. The china collects dirt and dust which is forever billowing in from the street. The shop is soulless. Tomb-like. I don't like it. I have asked Uncle Ely if we might add some large plants for color in the spring. He replied that it isn't a plant shop, and customers do not come to see plants and that was that. Perhaps I could persuade him to put a plant in the copper tub by the front door. The tub has not sold, and perhaps the plant would draw attention to it. I will attempt to return to the subject on another occasion when he is in a better humor.

Pansy

Sunday, 15 January 1905

Dear Diary,

Snow, snow and more snow! Canal Street continues to have just enough traffic to keep the road barely passable although sleds would fair far better than wheeled vehicles! Lispenard Street is virtually impassable. Once again, the weather has prevented an outing to church. This afternoon I have been huddled near the coal scuttle working my embroidery for the baby and watching Katy tumble about. Little Katy is a great comfort and companion to me. She gets stronger every day and is ever so amusing. She often hides under my bed or under my chair, but then darts out, chases her tail and tumbles all over and then hides again.

Uncle Ely has been spending almost all of his time in his back office. He has been quite preoccupied and not very communicative of late.

Bah! Will the winter ever end? Ah! Flossie has just come with more tea. Heaven!

Pansy

Monday, 16 January 1905

Dear Diary,

The snow tapered and turned to rain last night, and the streets were passable today. Uncle Ely is all astir, the shipment he sent from Mexico weeks ago has arrived in the city, and it is being delivered to the shop in a few days. He has been mumbling to himself, pacing, smoking his pipe and wringing his hands in anticipation for over a week. He says that the contents are exquisite specimens of Aztec culture and he has been clearing new floor space and display shelving in the shop to properly exhibit them. Flossie and I are apprehensive. We are already greatly discomforted by Uncle's existing collection. From what I have heard of the Aztecs, they were a cruel, bloodthirsty lot, and I would not care to have any objects belonging to them in my environs, but it seems to not trouble Uncle Ely in the slightest.

I attempted to broach the subject with him, to which he called me a silly child and waved a dismissive hand at me.

I worry about Uncle Ely's irreligious nature and irreverence. It is a strain to perceive how my dear, kind, God-fearing Papa could be the brother of this reticent man with the soul of a pirate, but I pray for him daily and am in gratitude that he has sheltered me. May God protect us and watch over us.

Pansy

Tuesday, 18 January 1905

Dear Diary,

Feeling restless and needing desperately to occupy myself, I recalled a box of memorabilia that mother kept which was full of letters and newspaper clippings. I found it in the bottom of a small trunk in the wardrobe. I had tucked it away when I first arrived, not wanting to have raw remembrances of Mamma and Papa. It was bittersweet to retrieve the box and peruse its contents. I have discovered a small bundle of yellowed letters and cards from Uncle Ely to Papa from the 1880s. They were stamped from various countries over a decade — Korea, China, India, Italy, Morocco, Portugal, England.

I knew that father had said Uncle Ely had gone abroad with the inheritance share he had received after grandfather's passing, but I had not the slightest inkling as to the extent of his travels! The letters were brief, mostly exalting the exotic locations, foods and interesting people he had encountered. There were quite a few from Italy which sounded more enthusiastic than the others. He mentioned a charming family he had found, and that he was contemplating staying on and securing regular employment. Following correspondence was more matter of fact 'Some streets and homes in Lisbon are hundreds of years old. One steps back in time here.' Another recounted how dreadfully seasick he had been on a long voyage aboard a steamship crossing the Atlantic, his constitution and spirit so low he hardly cared if he lived or died.

While his messages were concise and typically unsentimental, I still found it heart-warming to know that Uncle Ely had maintained contact with his younger brother during that time. While my father had married, bought a house, started a family, and ensconced himself in missionary work, his brother had chosen a path of wanderlust collecting and trading commodities from around the world. I am beginning to understand Uncle Ely a bit better. I have my own treasure box!

Pansy

Wednesday, 19 January 1905

Dear Diary,

Bartholomew has left us! This afternoon, a customer appeared in the shop, an older gentleman with a bad limp and British accent who said he had been an Army colonel overseas in Africa during the first Boer War. He paid handsomely for Bartholomew as well as for quite a few of the masks and spears. Flossie and I spent the afternoon wrapping the items for delivery tomorrow. This gentleman intends to decorate his library. We wonder if he aims to claim that he was the mighty hunter responsible for Bartholomew's demise! Flossie and I were elated to wrap the grotesque masks. How splendid they will no longer glower at us! We may actually miss Bartholomew however.

Pansy

Thursday, 19 January 1905

Dear Diary,

I have been so overwrought, I was simply unable to write until today. I believe I mentioned the shipment Uncle Ely was anticipating from Mexico. Late this morning, a heavy wagon arrived, and two men grunted and strained to deliver three substantial crates, each large enough to contain a full-grown man. The Djinni's Trove store front faces Canal Street but a separate service entrance off of Lispenard Street goes directly into the back office of the shop. Fortunately, although bleak and blustery today, we have had no precipitation, so it is fortuitous that these men did not have to contend with that additional hardship. Even with a wheeled cart, the men had great difficulty getting them through the door and all the way to the back office.

The shop office is a confined area to begin with, having just space for a wash basin and stand, the small safe, a long work bench that doubles as a desk and two large storage cabinets. These crates took up almost all the available floor space.

It took some time for Uncle Ely to open the first crate. He worked steadily around the first crate prying it open with a hammer and chisel. As he did so, he explained each crate contained large bundles wrapped in burlap packed in wood shavings. Once the top came loose, we dug through the shavings to the first bundle.

It was as wide as a church bench, roundish like a log and quite heavy. We lifted it out of the crate and onto the work bench. I carefully unwrapped the long bundle. It was wrapped up tightly like a mummy and took some time to unwind. It would have been more expedient to cut away at it with scissors, but Uncle Ely is very careful to keep materials like burlap and paper and twine in case he needs to wrap an object for transport, like poor Bartholomew. The last of the burlap fell away, and – how can I relate it? Before us lay a reclining man-creature with a large bowl on his stomach wolfishly grinning back at us! It had great bulging eyes and skeletal teeth in a wide grin. On its head was a great headpiece painted yellow, blue and red. This demonic object was made of terra cotta but was badly stained dark brown in uneven patches. The interior of the bowl was dark, dark brown, almost black. It smelled of earth and something else, something musty, rotten.

"This is ghastly!" I said backing away from it.

"It's perfect!" Uncle Ely responded. "Not a chip or crack. It's extremely valuable. I intend to sell it to the Natural History Museum! They have plans for expansion. This collection is going to make me a *lot* of money!" He clapped his hands together in glee.

He set the bowl-bearing creature on one of the shelves and we pulled out the next object. This was large and flat like a table top. It too was very tightly wrapped and was quite difficult to maneuver because of its weight. It took some time to unbind as well. This was revealed to be a large mask with empty eye sockets, and a large mouth in a skeletal grin. It had small blood-red gem stones around the eyes and nose. Writhing like a snake through the eye sockets and mouth was a thin blue line like smoke. It was horrid. My hands trembled as I removed the last of the wrappings.

"This one is a God, they said. Completely unpronounceable Tezcat-something. Supposed to be smoke coming out of him. Fantastic specimen!" Uncle Ely beamed. We leaned this against a cabinet.

He went on to say that he'd want to mount this on the wall opposite the front door. It would be quite eye-catching upon entering the shop, he argued with mirth.

"Might it not frighten your customers away?" I asked.

"Nonsense, child!" he said then explained that he believed customers who come to a curio shop are expecting to see something lurid, something dark, something foreboding. That's why freak shows are so popular! A person with a minor deformity is just unfortunate, but a person with fish scales and a tail why, that begs to be seen! The more bizarre, the better! Sadly, I had to agree with his observation.

"Just wait to you see the rest of the collection, my dear, it is simply magnificent." He pulled a smaller bundle out of the first crate. The bundle contained several pamphlets he said he picked up in Mexico and thought would be invaluable in cataloging the collection. They describe some of the Aztec culture and artifacts.

He tossed the bundle on the workbench next to me. On the cover of the first pamphlet was a crest of an eagle balanced gingerly on a cactus. The eagle's wings were outstretched, its mouth open as if crying out, and its sharp claws barely touching the tips of the spiky cactus.

I examined this pamphlet. The topics ranged from the style of houses and diet of the Aztecs, to their advanced knowledge of medicines and education. It struck me as very peculiar that on the one hand they were a violent society exalting their champion warriors and waging war with neighboring cultures, while on the other hand, they valued education and arts excelling in crafts and weaving as well as in fabricating jewelry, ceremonial breastplates and the like.

Uncle Ely had pulled out another large bundle. "You'll like this, Pansy, it's a collection of jewelry." He set the bundle on the work bench for me to unwrap. He stepped back and watched me. This bundle was lighter and was bound in twine like a package. I removed the twine and slowly unwrapped the paper. It contained several smaller bundles. The first was a gold medallion, just larger than my hand. Inlaid in the center was a magnificent crouching jaguar, its spots raised bits of obsidian set in turquoise.

Gazing on this exquisite artifact, holding it in my hands was indescribable. It was mesmerizing in its beauty and refinement. I could not pull my eyes away from it. I could understand for a moment why my uncle chose to travel the world in pursuit of treasures and oddities. To search and search and one day to find something with this grandeur and to own it! I thought of the travelers who had gone out west in search of gold who would have celebrated a raw little pebble of a nugget. There I stood holding this spectacular item in my hand.

"You see, Pansy," he said gently, still looking at my face, "Isn't it utterly amazing?" He took it from me gently, setting it aside and designating that it would go in the safe.

The rest of that bundle was an odd assortment of combs, buckles, rings, and tools inlaid with stones. All were impressive, but the medallion was by far the greatest treasure. My apprehension of this collection was beginning to subside. Flossie appeared in the doorway and announced that supper was ready, so we adjourned to the dining room. The weather outside remains bleak and it very well may snow tonight. The heavy drapes sway like phantoms from the frigid drafts.

Pansy

Friday, 20 January 1905

Dear Diary,

Reverend Hargrove and his wife, Elizabeth called on us this morning. Uncle Ely does not attend church except on a rare occasion, but I attempt to attend whenever possible. They said they were visiting friends nearby and thought to stop in as they were concerned that I had not been in attendance these past two Sundays. Flossie brought us tea and some biscuits and we had a nice visit. Fortunately, they did not stay long. While I greatly appreciated their thoughtfulness, and normally find their company quite pleasant, I was keenly aware that Uncle Ely would far rather be in his shop unpacking his crates. He made a minimal effort to be civil and participate in the banter.

I prayed the Hargroves were not cognizant of the tension in the parlor. Further adding to the discomfort, Reverend and Mrs. Hargrove reiterated how lovely it would be to see more of Uncle Ely in church. I knew this overture would not be warmly received. Upon their departure, Elizabeth clasped my hands warmly and said, "You are constantly in our prayers, dear. Let us know if we can ever be of service to you." I thanked her, and they took their leave.

Sometime after lunch, I went to down to the shop to check on Uncle Ely's progress. I pushed through the curtain between the shop and the back office to find Uncle Ely between two hideous monsters. I could not suppress my shriek, as for a moment I judged that Uncle Ely was truly in peril. He stood between them, each almost half his height, being of blackest obsidian, the male composed of a skull with staring orbs with no eyelids, his ribs exposed, and beneath his ribs, his giant heart and stomach cavity wide open. His legs reduced to skeletal feet. His neck was adorned with necklaces of skulls, and his arms were outstretched, as if reaching up to be held by Uncle Ely.

On the right was a similar being with pendulous breasts dropping over her exposed ribs and heart, and her headdress was adorned with tiny bodies writhing in torment with minute blades in their chest forms. She too was reaching out with skeletal arms to Uncle Ely. It was as if they had come from hell itself to escort Uncle Ely back down with them.

I fought not to swoon but had to lean against the bench for support. It was then that I saw the final horror. Another large, squatting, staring demon with huge round empty eyes, also with a headdress adorned with tiny tortured bodies, their supplicating hands raised to heaven, their mouths open screaming. This despicable thing was of a lighter stone yet was stained dark brown in a rough pattern like a shawl. From it floated the smell of stale smoke and rot, like the smell of a dead rat and the worst tenement sewage. The evil that pulsed from it reached out to me, and I fainted dead away.

God protect us from this evil!

Pansy

Monday, 23 January 1905

Dear Violet,

It is with regret that I relate the news regarding the state of your sister's health. I am at a loss as to what to do, and hope that perhaps you would be able to come as soon as possible. Pansy has been suffering these past few days with a terrible fever. Doctor Whitney came yesterday and believes it was brought on by the cold and by acute distress. Regrettably I fear I am to blame. Pansy was kindly assisting me with some new acquisitions which are, I must admit rather gruesome in appearance, and she came upon them without any forewarning of their macabre visages. She fainted. She recovered briefly but then weakened and was overcome with fever. Flossie has been tending to her, but the fever is causing some perturbing nightmares which are frightening Flossie, and she has become quite irrational. You have a level head, and I feel that your presence may be of great comfort to Pansy. Please come at once if your devoted husband can spare you.

Yours faithfully,

Uncle Ely

Wednesday, 25 January 1905

My darling Raymond,

I scarcely know where to begin. I arrived at Uncle's house yesterday afternoon to find Pansy still gripped with fever. Since her original onset of yellow fever as a small child, I have been bedside with her through several maladies, and yet this one seems distressingly prolonged and aggressive. She sleeps mostly but fitfully, tossing and writhing on the bed as if in great torment. She perspires profusely despite all efforts to apply cool cloths to her brow and regularly wiping down her arms and legs. She moans and cries out, as if in a sustained nightmare. She rambles names that do not sound like English and mumbles about drumming and blood, always the blood. Flossie, who has always been a bit of a silly mouse is nigh on hysterical and useless. Uncle Ely was quite right to send for me.

This morning I asked Uncle Ely to describe to me in detail what had occurred prior to this appalling attack. He described to me the artifacts he had selected in Mexico City near the old main city of the Aztecs, Tenochtitlan. These artifacts it would appear, were from an archaeological site (I dared not ask exactly how he came to acquire them as I suspect it was not entirely or strictly legal – father often mentioned a certain fogginess and circumspection regarding Uncle Ely's stories of how he comes upon his treasured finds.) The largest of them depict Aztec gods, and most of those seemed to demand blood sacrifices. I had not been in Uncle Ely's shop in quite some time, and he gave me a brief tour, ending in the back room, where he had uncased these figures. Never in my life have I beheld such hideous possessions. I was immensely grateful for his explanatory prelude, or like Pansy, I may too have been frightened out of my senses. I could not stay in their presence and had to withdraw. Uncle Ely handed me the pamphlets with notes regarding their 'identities' and original purpose.

The horror which I will relate is by no means verging on exaggeration, I take this information directly from the pamphlets. I will only tell you the very worst of the lot, as there are many smaller horrors as well such as fanged serpents, snarling monkeys, fierce eagles with needle-sharp claws extended --these seem like quaint baubles in comparison to what I will attempt to relate to you.

There is a vessel called a 'chac-mool' which in appearance is a ghoulish skeleton man reclining with a bowl on his stomach, a bowl which was used to hold the still beating heart of a sacrifice once it was cut and removed from his chest, and oh, yes, this does indeed bare the stains, dark stains in a dreadful splatter, an irregular, splotchy pattern that has all the signs of dried blood.

Chac-mool

There are two statues with arms outstretched before them, like large children, but again freakishly lacking any other childlike attributes of innocence or charm; no, these are demonic skeletons bedecked with necklaces of skulls, wearing great colorful helmets with tiny suffering beings crying out for help, blades protruding from their minute chests. They are both posed as if about to step forward. One is male, the other female. These are the Deities of Death: Mictlantecuhtli and his wife Mictecacihautl. Symbols related to them include spiders, owls and bats. They are said to reside in a windowless house and require frequent sacrifices to continue the cycle of life.

The worst of the lot is a dreadful squatting troll with a skeleton body, vacant staring eyes and grinning teeth. In scale, it is as large as your nephew, Hugh. It has a particularly disagreeable aura about it: threatening, needy and *hungry*. Yes, I know that sounds fanciful, but there it is all the same. Hungry and needy.

The booklet identifies this as Xipe Totec a God who required flesh and blood. The poor victims who were sacrificed to this God — if you can really call such a being a God, it seems all twisted, this horrid demanding God-- were flayed alive, and the strips of flesh were laid upon this hideous thing like a great coat! So yes, this very thing sitting, grinning in the rooms below this very dwelling were once draped, sickly adorned with the flesh of countless humans!

Is it any wonder that walking into this shadowy room and encountering such horrors, my poor dear sister Pansy collapsed? Uncle Ely says he is making arrangements for some men from the Museum of Natural History to come view this unholy collection in the hopes that they will buy it for their Central American exhibit. Pray God this comes to pass swiftly! I've noticed that even Uncle Ely has been uncharacteristically saturnine after spending a lengthy time in that office. I worry that the exposure to such forces of malevolence is ill affecting him.

Pansy is screaming again and twisting in her bed sheets, and it seems that no matter how much coal Flossie adds to the fire, we can't get this room warm enough. I must go.

Your loving wife,

Violet

Friday, 27 January 1905

My beloved Raymond,

It has been snowing all day, with great howling gusts of wind. One cannot see beyond the lamp post by the front window it snows so earnestly. It would be charming if we were together in a cozy house by a great fire, but here in this house, this room with poor Pansy fading in and out, it is beyond confining. Doctor Whitney was able to come again yesterday and was hopeful that her fever was reduced and she was calm, but an attack came on again before dawn this morning.

Pansy cried out, "Oh, so much blood!" and "the steps, the steps, the bloody steps!" Once she sat straight up in the bed, opened her eyes and yelled, "They are fighting over the arms and legs to take home and eat!" I cannot describe fully what effect these ghastly outbursts have had upon me. She collapsed back into the pillow moaning again. These attacks usually last for about a quarter of an hour and it takes me twice that to recover my own composure.

Pansy has always been small and meek to behold, but even as a child she had a quiet inner strength, perhaps due to her unflappable faith. I pray that she will resist whatever this illness is and return to us unscathed.

Flossie has told me that for weeks there have been crows each morning cawing at Pansy's window, causing her extreme agitation. I wanted to dismiss this as superstition, but now I too have seen them. Even this morning, with the whipping snow, there were three crows raucously cawing. Flossie says the shoe shop owner has paid boys to throw rocks at them to no avail; they keep coming back.

Uncle Ely has been more disagreeable and sullen. He does not come to meals and spends most of his time in that back room of the shop. I thought he was preparing the Aztec collection for the museum people, but I do not see what occupies all his time. The items are all unpacked and ready for display. One would have thought him to be more jovial in anticipation of the potential sale, which would increase his fortune most admirably. Inexplicably quite the reverse seems to be transpiring. He would argue with his morning coffee I think, if he were taking breakfast. With the snow, surely his museum people will not be able to come so we might be free of those fearsome things, though I doubt the delay is the cause of his ill temper.

This morning after breakfast, what with such a difficult morning, Flossie and I lost track of Pansy's kitten. We searched for it all over the house but did not find it. Reluctantly, oh Raymond, so reluctantly, I went downstairs. The inner door between the house and the shop was open ajar, and as I got closer, I heard poor kitten, she let loose with the loudest hiss of any full-sized cat and came bolting into the house. Little Katy's hair was straight up all over, and her eyes were huge. Something had frightened her terribly. She had difficulty getting back up the stairs and cried most pitiably. I scooped her up in my hands and she was trembling awfully! I took her back upstairs to Pansy's room and put her in her slipper by the fire. What could have frightened her so? I dare not contemplate, lest my imagination get the best of me.

Your loving wife,

Violet

Sunday, 29, January 1905

My beloved Raymond,

It was about two o'clock this morning. I had fallen asleep next to Pansy's bed. I had had an awful dream with voices calling out and remember seeing so many people all looking at me expectantly. I felt tired and confused, and they were ushering me forward. All I could see was red. The walkway was red, and I slipped. When I awoke, the room was terribly cold and I called for Flossie to bring up more coal. Pansy's eyes opened slowly and she looked at me. She pulled her arm from the coverlet and reached for my hand. She was so weak; her eyes were hardly open. I put my ear to her mouth and she said, "Vi -- Vio-let. You must get out. You are in...

great...danger." Her lips seemed very dry. I went to the pitcher and poured a small glass of water. It was so cold in the room, I thought I saw ice forming in the pitcher. I made Pansy sip the water. She licked her lips and said again. "Violet. You must get out."

"Dear Pansy, you've had a terrible fever. I am well, and you will be too, you just need to rest and--" Pansy interrupted me by grabbing my arm with more force than I would have suspected her of being capable, like the grip of a bird of prey.

"Violet. We need help." She fell back to the pillow and her eyes closed. Pansy was calm for a time, her breath coming in slow rhythmic intervals. I was hopeful that the tide was turning. Flossie arrived with more coal, and with much effort the room warmed a bit. I fell asleep in the chair.

"Miss Violet! Miss Violet!" I looked up to find Flossie hovering over me with concern.

"What is it?" I glanced at Pansy. She looked feverish again and was murmuring something.

"You were both at it!" Flossie said. "She was moaning about the blood, and so were you! It frightened me something awful!"

I was so exhausted, I couldn't remember what I had dreamed. My stomach hurt a bit and I felt some morning sickness coming on. I asked for some water. Flossie brought me a glass of water, and I asked what time it was. It was after nine o'clock. I inquired if Uncle Ely had been up for breakfast.

"I don't know. I've not seen him this morning. He may have spent the night in the shop," she said.

I dressed slowly and asked Flossie to fix us some breakfast. Pansy was conscious, and we got her to take some bites of toast and some weak tea. As she had before, she pulled me to her. I put my ear to her mouth.

"Check on Uncle Ely. He has to be gotten out of the shop." I glanced to Flossie, and nodded to Pansy, yes, we'd go check on

Uncle Ely.

I still felt so weak, and yet I sensed an urgency. Something was very wrong about those Aztec objects and it was affecting all of us. Flossie and I moved slowly downstairs. We opened the connecting door to the curio shop and stepped inside. There were no lights on in the front display room. I called out, "Uncle Ely?" There was no response. It was so cold we could see our breath. We moved to the back and parted the dividing curtain.

There were no lights on, but through the gloom, we could see that Uncle Ely was lying on the floor between the two standing figures. There was a halo of blood around his head. Flossie screamed. We ran to him and wrestled him from between the statues. The coals were gray in the fireplace, the fire had died away some time ago. The child size fiend-figures on either side of Uncle Ely appeared to reach for us. The squatting ghoul on the table above us grinned as if mocking us. Fear would have paralyzed me completely if I had not been compelled to revive Uncle Ely. We struggled to get him to a sitting position, then up onto our shoulders and out of the shop. This was no minor accomplishment as he is a bulky man and was offering no assistance to us. Flossie was immeasurably helpful, being heavy-boned and quite strong, not like Pansy or myself. She took most of the weight of him while I kept us steady. It was doubtful we would have gotten him up the stairs, but all of our tugging and pulling must have awakened him, for he did come around mumbling, and he was able to take some steps with us.

We were not sure what caused his injury. There seems to be a gash on his forehead as if he had fallen on something yet had a second wound on his stomach and if poked by a sharp instrument. We had not seen any object near him that might have caused these lacerations. It was most peculiar. Fortunately, neither injury was very grave, we were able to clean and dress his wounds fairly easily once we got him to his bed. We got him to take some beef tea. He was very weak and mumbled incoherently, although I thought one phrase sounded like "they came at me."

Mrs. Cross and her nephew Wyatt stopped by after church to check on Pansy. I explained that Uncle Ely had had a fall, but that I thought Pansy was slowly on the mend. We had been talking just a little while when Pansy surprised me utterly by appearing in the doorway. She was dressed and had even tidied her hair. She came in and sat down. Wyatt looked shocked to see how pale and frail she was, and Mrs. Cross fluttered about how awful it was that she had been so ill. Seeing what a toll it was taking on Pansy to be sociable, they did not stay long. We hugged them, and they departed.

"Pansy!" I chastised, "You shouldn't be up and about!"

"There is no time to lose." She said. "I have slipped a note to Wyatt. He will invent an errand to run to escape Mrs. Cross, and he will be back as quickly as possible. I simply wrote, "We need your help. Utter discretion required. Please return alone at once."

She continued, "Listen, Violet, I have seen it clearly and can scarcely bear it. We are all in danger as long as those horrid things are about. They've gone after Uncle Ely, but they really want *you*." I was struck dumb by her intensity and conviction.

"Didn't you have dreams?" she pressed me. "Didn't you see the steps of the Aztec temple, and the blood running down? The victims being dragged up? The ceremonial drums beating incessantly?"

I felt my stomach where my new baby was and felt a sharp pain. I recalled the dreams-- the screaming, the drums. Worse, I had a flash of a warrior figure jumping around before me with a head dress of large feathers and a great beak over his brow. He had a chest plate that also bore a fierce eagle on it.

"Violet," she continued, "I know those things are worth a fortune money-wise, but you have to see they are not safe. Even if Uncle Ely gets them out of the house and to a museum, then what? Then how many more people will be exposed to their demonic and insatiable need for blood?"

"Pansy," I started, "This all seems so fanciful --" I wanted to be rational and sensible, but even as I questioned her, I knew that somehow, we had crossed into a different realm.

"Violet" she persisted. "Did you read the pamphlets? You know that not all the captured people from neighboring areas were killed as sacrifices, right? Some of them were kept as slaves. Some of them became entertainment and had to play ball games to win or die. They were sorted like vegetables in a market, Violet. If they were old, scarred, ugly, they were not considered worthy to be offered up to the hungry Gods. That would be insulting to offer up something imperfect, do you see? The old, the ugly and so on became slaves in the fields, or in their violent games, and who cared if they died? They would be killed anyway if they lost. If they won, they just had to play again and eventually die. The beautiful ones, though, the perfect ones --" she paused, and looked at my belly, "the innocent, unblemished ones, were the best offerings." She had tears welling in her eyes. "Oh, my dearest, they want you, Violet, but they want your baby most of all."

We went to check on Uncle Ely and asked Flossie to bring him more beef tea. Pansy slipped a sleeping draught into his cup when Flossie wasn't looking.

Wyatt arrived about three quarters of an hour later. We did not disclose to him everything but gave him the overview and swore him to secrecy. He went away again and returned with a tremendous sledge hammer. He said he had found some men with a horse wagon who would come around shortly. Wyatt and I walked into the Djinni's Trove together, Pansy and Flossie following us. Pansy was reading aloud from the Book of Psalms. We pulled back the dividing drapery and entered the back room. While Flossie and Pansy and I all said prayers, Wyatt set the chac-mool down on the floor. We covered it in burlap so the pieces would not fly all over the shop, or us. When it was completely covered, and while we continued with prayers for deliverance from evil and a blessing on this place, Wyatt hefted the sledge hammer and let it come down again and again until there were no more shapes bubbling under the burlap.

Next, the shield of Tezcatlipoca was placed flat and covered completely. Did we hear something like air escaping? Was that a wisp of smoke that curled up from the floor? Again and again the sledge came down. Did we see the statues of the Gods of Death take a step back? I only saw Wyatt hesitate a moment. I'm fairly certain he saw what we saw. He blinked several times as if to clear his eyes, glanced at me, then Pansy, then commenced smashing with renewed vigor.

Did I hear the drumming only in my head, or was it really in the room? The Gods of Death were laid down side by side and covered completely and the sledge came down again and again. Did the crouching figure snarl at us, or was that a strange shadow? Finally, it too was set down, and imagination or no, I heard snarling and even more repugnant, I thought I felt it pulling away from us as we grabbed it by the arms. This also was quickly — dare I say it, subdued? Like the others, it was covered and smashed. Next, we bagged all the bits, every last one. We were sweeping the dust into bags and secured them tightly with twine. We were almost finished when I passed my broom beneath the work bench and heard a metal sound. My broom snared two knives I recognized from the glass cabinet upstairs in the parlor. They were the perfect size for child sized hands. Flossie and I stared at them in disbelief. Each had a brown stain on the blade. Picking them up gingerly I set them on the work bench to clean and replace upstairs later. Flossie mopped the area with a rag and washed the remaining rag dust down the sink.

It was just after dusk when the horse wagon arrived. Wyatt told the men that we had dismantled a bricked-up archway and just needed to remove the debris. He directed them to take the bundles along Canal Street and dump the bags into the Hudson River. He paid each of them, and they readily loaded up the bundles and took them away. As they were pulling away, Pansy and Wyatt exchanged a look, and Wyatt went with the men, just to be sure the job was properly accomplished.

It is so late, but I had to relate it all. It is done. I plan to be on the train home after lunch tomorrow. It seems an eternity since I have held you in my embrace.

Your devoted wife,

Violet

Friday, 3 February 1905

Dear Violet,

Uncle Ely is recovering nicely from his wounds, and rather more remarkable, has recovered his temperament. I was fearful as to how to relate to Uncle Ely what transpired, dreading a volcanic reaction when I had to inform him that his prize pieces from his Aztec artifacts had been smashed to bits, but I suspect that whatever happened to Uncle Ely in that office (he steadfastly keeps his own council as to what took place) he was not sorry to learn of their utter destruction. Rather, his face relaxed and his head fell back to the pillow. He surprised me by thanking me and asking me to thank you as well. Imagine my relief!

Two gentlemen are expected from the museum tomorrow morning, and will be presented with the smaller pieces, the medallion, the combs etc. Uncle Ely feels confident that they will be pleased to have the medallion in their collection, and it alone will enhance his finances most adequately.

He has apologized again for his mysterious behavior these last weeks and has been more kind and open hearted than I have ever seen him. He even promised that Flossie could take this Sunday off. He has also relented and allowed that a few living plants in the choice locations in the shop might be a welcomed addition and attract the shopper's eye to nearby objects of interest.

Best of all, while Uncle Ely was recovering and his manner was soft, I beseeched him to disclose to me why he had never married. He sighed, held my hand in his, and related that yes, in fact, when he was in his early twenties and travelling, he was enamored of a girl, Marianne, whose family ran a bakery in a small town in Italy. She was a simple girl, but gentle and kind. He would have found work and stayed there forever if they had had the good fortune to be united in matrimony. Just as it seemed that perhaps her family would approve of their union, a great tragedy occurred. Marianne was out on a walk in the countryside and was attacked by a pack of wild dogs. She fell and suffered deep bites all over her body. The wounds refused to heal and became terribly infected. A high fever developed. She died a slow tormented death. Uncle Ely and her father found the dogs and killed them all, but naturally it could not bring back his beloved Marianne. Broken hearted and miserable that he had not been there to save her, Uncle Ely put his attentions into collecting artifacts and setting up a name for himself and an import business.

Perhaps you and I might set our minds to matchmaking?

Your devoted sister,

Pansy

P.S. We've not seen any crows on the ledge since Wyatt and the men went about their business, and I slept in late this morning with glorious dreams of Coney Island.

Note

I dedicate this to Peter, Jean and Ro who got me through the hardest and longest consecutive three years of my life: my Lion, Scarecrow and if Dorothy had a lost twin…and Marie who saw the cat too…saw it for something other.

This one really happened.

The Black Cat

My folks shipped me off to a boarding school when I was fourteen. Our local high school had a "milquetoast principal" and a shoddy reputation, and my mother had high hopes of prepifying me, turning me into a plaid-loving, tennis-playing, well rounded catch for a New England doctor or lawyer.

Perhaps I'm a changeling, switched at birth for the child she really wanted to mold.

The education was exceptional, I will say that but socially, it was like living in a pressure cooker. Anyone who was ever shipped off to summer camp and didn't have a ripping good time of it can imagine how boarding school has all the potentials of the worst day in high school without the respite of going home. I attended for three years, only leaving campus for one weekend besides the allotted holidays.

At least my parents conceded this point: I got to attend a co-educational school. My mother had fixated on an all-girls' school, but I balked, hugely relieved when I was accepted at K----. The only centipede in the bubble-bath was that the girls' campus was five miles up a mountain from the boys', and while buses ran up and down all day, classes were hardly 50/50. I had three boys in my

English class on the mountain, and I was one of two girls in my Latin class in the valley. The big social occasion was the Saturday night movie. After dinner, girls were dutifully bused, like cattle, to the movie option at the campus theatre down the mountain.

We disembarked in a wide parking lot corralled by stone walls and the river. To get to the theatre, we walked through a gauntlet of boys and male teachers, following a path that narrowed and wound in front of the dorms and the classroom buildings to the far side of the quad. This gave ample opportunity for jeering, cat calling and other mob behaviors, with the ambiance of being herded to an auction block.

And to get through all of that to see *Apocalypse Now,* can I just say, was hardly a treat.

But the other option was to stay in a gray, cinder block dormitory and watch television. This was way before cable or satellite; I think the television got five channels.

If a girl was lucky enough to have a boyfriend, there wasn't much chance to spend time with him. We had classes six days a week, required chapel four times a week, and even if you met up, there was nowhere to go to have a private moment. Common rooms on the opposite campuses were verboten and winter in Connecticut is long. You can get frostbite walking around looking for a private spot behind a building. Necking in the chapel seemed just wrong, although I'm sure lots took place there after hours. The chapel, made of slate and stone, maintains a lovely morgue-like temperature on the warmest of days. Still, it was shelter from wind, rain and snow, and did have shadowy corners.

I'm sure it's different now, but at the time, any infraction of the rules incurred a small work project, for one to three hours in duration. Shoveling snow, scraping gum from under dining hall chairs, extra dish crew, washing black boards, raking leaves. If you didn't report to hours, you got more hours.

My slate was clean; I'm dim to the full array of tasks readily dispensed. For the most part, this system made sense, and was pretty successful at keeping students in line. There were a few rebellious ones who racked up ridiculous numbers of hours with no intention of completing them. Expulsion was an option infrequently forced into action.

But here was the cruel part: seniors were allowed to bestow hours on underlings. This meant that a senior with a grudge could assign you a work project just for seeing you, happily inventing your trespass: walking on the grass, not wearing proper uniform or the all-purpose, "insubordination."

Smart and power hungry seniors abused this privilege mightily. I learned early on to avoid seniors when in town, often ducking into the graveyard, even hiding behind tall grave markers. I wondered about a woman named Lovicy who was buried next to three husbands. Peachy-keen for her, if she loved them, but kind of weird for them, no? Buried with strangers who had loved the same woman?

Aside from heaps of homework…French papers, Latin translations and, I'm not kidding, Dickens' *Our Mutual Friend* in English class. In paperback it's at least an inch and a half thick and has 72 characters. Yeah. Fun keeping track of that without a chart. And let's not forget the mandatory meals; if you skipped lunch that's a three hour work project, just in case you needed the exercise.

Daily routine: Wake up before dawn, select one of three uniform options you have. Sign in at breakfast. Class all morning, sign in at lunch, class until four. Change clothes, go to your required sport. Change back into uni for dinner. Homework all night. Bed check at 10:30 PM. Repeat, repeat repeat. Wednesday and Saturday half days, *woo-hoo!* But at some point, you had laundry to address. Two campuses of students storming the Laundromat at the end of town. Feeding quarters to that dryer once you landed a free one sucked up all that free time. You had to be on the bus at 5 PM too, or of course there'd be hours for missing the bus and being off-campus.

And there was always more homework than time.

I knew two girls who had fathers with terminal illnesses. Each hoped but did not expect their father to live long enough to see them graduate. Some evenings we could hear them crying down the hall, or sobbing in the pay phone at the bottom of the stairwell. One particularly bitchy senior decided to assign hours to a girl for being on the phone after curfew, a seniors-only privilege. This sparked a screaming match and near brawl. Fortunately, the Dean wisely made an allowance for the distressed caller.

This was our world. Structured, repressed, and isolated on top of a mountain that had its own weather. Weather that was just wild in the early winter; wind sweeping angry clouds across the moon at night, sudden violent storms with strobe-light-style lightning, and leaves blowing all the time.

On nights when the wind howled and waves flitted across the little pond out front, my roommate, Jean and I would sneak out to feel the power of it. We'd run up to the empty field by the road and watch the clouds and stand against the intensity of the gusts. There's something primal and invigorating about stomping out into the storm, the wind, the wild night.

I always felt there was something in the woods. Something watching us.

It was not surprising to me when I struck up a conversation about ghosts with a girl in the riding program who told me that odd things were sometimes found on the horse trails. She said on one riding path that went down the mountain, there was a small clearing with tree stumps arranged in a circle. Each stump had a candle nub on it, burned down to its base.

She'd heard they'd found a severed goat head on the path once. Another time a dead cat. And once, dead crows hung upside down like freakish wind chimes suspended from the trees over the stump circle.

Wiccans might practice in the woods, but they don't use animal sacrifices. This was dark magick, confirming for me there was a weird energy in the woods.

My mother, a bird lover, hated cats. My first experience with a cat was all purring until it hissed and raked its claws down my arm leaving red streamers of blood. So I'll confess, at the time, I was not a cat fan.

I noticed the black cat on the rock wall one day as we were walking to breakfast; a sleek, onyx black cat I'd never seen before. It put the hair up on my neck at once. It looked very intelligent. It looked like it was watching us, studying us, taking notes. Not a casual observation, a careful study. I watched its eyes pan the group in front of us. The eyes reached us. Gold eyes. We locked eyes. It jumped down and ran away.

This became a pattern. Pan, pan, pan, see me, break and run. Morning, afternoon, evening. My friends reluctantly agreed that it was eerie and by no means my imagination.

You'll think I'm hopelessly egocentric and exaggerating, but I think not, you'll see. Something about this cat gave me the heebie-jeebies right from the start. And it wasn't the only cat, there were plenty of odd cats, cats that had wandered from the stable and made a breakaway group. No doubt they found their way to the trash behind the dining hall. And bred.

But this black cat was something else. Something not normal.

About the fifth time we played this spy game, I felt it was looking for me. Possibly others too, but I was a target. So the next morning, walking with two other girls towards the dining hall, I said, "I want you to watch something. As we approach the dining hall, you will likely see a black cat. He will appear to be looking for someone. I will bet that when he spots me, he will run away."

Sure enough. My friends confirmed that it was eerie and by no means my imagination. They agreed. This became a pattern. Pan, pan, pan, see me, break and run. Morning, afternoon, evening.

Things escalated.

At night, walking to the library, I got the skin-crawling feeling that I was being watched. There were few street lights back then, so a large circle of light would almost blind one who was then plunged back into darkness for a lengthy stretch before the next circle of light ahead. As I got closer to, but not in the circle of light, I looked back to see movement, and there it was. A black shadow creeping along the wall behind me, coming to a stop just after I did. I walked. It walked. I stopped. It stopped. I trotted to the schoolhouse eager to find other students.

One windy night, Jean and I were walking to the schoolhouse to cram for a math exam, wanting to use the white board in an empty classroom and spread our notes out on the teacher's desk.

Halfway there we got the creepies.

The tree limbs around us bent and swayed throwing crazy patterns of shadows on the road. I recall trudging, a dragging feeling of text books weighting me down. Glancing back, I caught a glimpse of the silent black shadow loping along behind us. I whispered to Jean. Did she see it too? Yes.

We crossed the circle of light. I saw motion in the darkness behind us, black-hole dark in the night dark.

I'd had a bad day, and felt fed up with it all, the homework, the stress, the bitchy, taunting girls, the damn blue polyester skirt and now this sneaking, skulking cat. I worked up my mojo to a place so angry that I had no fear. I let the book bag drop to the ground with a thunk. I turned fully and faced the cat. Its eyes gleamed in the darkness just outside the circle of light, waiting.

Jean started to speak, "What are you doing? We should just keep moving—"

I'd had enough and was ready to scream, so I did.

"IF YOU ARE ANYTHING OTHER THAN A CAT, REVEAL YOURSELF FOR WHAT YOU TRULY ARE! SHOW YOURSELF RIGHT NOW!"

Note: If you are ever confronted with something supernatural, I don't recommend this tactic unless you know what you are doing and have a contingency plan.

I was utterly unprepared for what happened next.

The black cat trotted out of the shadow straight to me cutting a black radius into the circle of light. It hunched at my feet, looked up at me and hissed, that full on kind of angry, spitting, all teeth exposed hiss. "What do you think I am?" it seemed to ask.

We ran like hell.

It ran along right behind us.

If anyone had seen us that night from a distance, I'm sure we looked like lunatics, two girls running and screaming like hell was behind them.

I think it was.

We got to the glass door of the schoolhouse and pulled it shut behind us. The cat, close on our heels, stopped short of slamming into the pane. It looked up and hissed staring straight at us. It began pacing back and forth against the door yowling that piercing and tortured, cat-in-heat sound that puts ice crystals in your spine.

We ran into the farthest classroom we could find and stayed there for a long time.

We'd have to be back for the room check. We tiptoed to the outer door and peered out. Nothing. I stepped outside a few feet scanning the bushes and grass for movement. Jean was ready at the door if I spotted it and needed to run back. Nothing. I signaled to Jean and we speed walked back to our dorm.

A good three weeks passed, and no black cat. The tension of looking out for it eased. I began to relax. Maybe it was gone.

Not quite. I saw it one last time.

For a change, some entertainment was planned for the girls' campus. A live band was going to perform for a dance at the gym and the boys were to be bussed up the mountain. This must have been in the spring, because it was after dinner and yet still light outside as the buses arrived. Jean and I walked over from the dorm to meet our boyfriends. Quite a crowd of students milled about in the entryway, but I spotted Peter from a distance.

He was supporting something in his arms. At first, I thought it might be a gift for me.

From about ten feet away I recognized the furry black bundle. It was cradled with its face away from me, looking over Peter's shoulder.

I stopped short, frozen. "Put the cat down."

"No, it's a sweet kitty, I wanted to show it to you."

"Put the cat down."

"But I *love* cats. Cats are great. This one really likes me. I saw it when I got off the bus. It came to me and let me pick it up like it was waiting for me. He's just been purring up a storm."

How in the world had the cat found him? I fought to stay calm and not cause a scene.

Jean was frozen next to me, her voice jittery. "Uh, no, really, she's right."

"LOOK! It's a sweet kitty. Here, hold it," Peter insisted.

At this point he turned the cat around to face us, and the cat and I locked eyes. This knowing feeling swept over me that it had picked Peter on purpose. I don't know how or why, but it knew somehow. Of all the people, five busloads of boys and most of the girls' campus standing around, what were the chances? For the microsecond before it hissed, spazzed and ran away behind the gym, it stared at me. Smug. Gloating.

I never saw it after that. Perhaps it was just a cranky cat and the rest was all projection and imagination, a product of stress and the repressive atmosphere.

Or it was a familiar that got called home by its owner. Or it became a sacrifice.

If by chance you've sent your child off to K----, not to worry. As you know, the girl's campus was sold off decades ago, the campuses merged. My teachers are basking in retirement. There are co-ed common rooms and lounges aplenty, and I'd guess they've even dropped the dress code by now.

However, if your child is in the riding program, which may still be on the mountain, you might want to warn him or her to be wary of the woods.

And don't pick up any black cats.

Note

I've thrown some epic Halloween parties, and despite elaborate and expensive props, the most comments/compliments were over silly kid jokes written on orange pumpkin-shaped construction paper stuck at random on doors, walls, and windows.

When is a turkey like a ghost?

When it's a poultrygeist!

Silly, yes, but it makes me laugh just to say poultrygeist. So I had to come up with a story for it.

Poultrygeist

INTERESTING FACTS ABOUT TURKEYS:

The fleshy business over a male's beak is called a snood.

Turkeys have over 20 distinct vocalizations, and each turkey has a unique voice recognizable by other turkeys.

For a short distance, a wild turkey is capable of running over 20 miles an hour, and flying over 50 miles an hour.

Turkeys roost in trees.

Turkeys are very social, creating lasting bonds.

Turkeys are territorial to the degree that they can orient themselves over 1,000 acres.

Ghost turkeys will not give up their old stomping grounds without a BIG fight.

INTERESTING FACTS ABOUT CHICKENS:

Chickens can recognize each other, other animals, and humans.

As with turkeys, hens as well as roosters can be aggressive.

The spurs on a rooster continue to grow and are extremely hard, like metal spikes.

It is difficult to reason with poultry. Only a very adept psychic can convince a pissed off bird to go to the white light.

I ran into Charlie in a grocery store outside Charlotte two years ago. We were close to a coffee shop, so we put our groceries in our cars and walked over. I ordered a small latte and he ordered a small black coffee. We sat down at a table outside.

I hadn't seen him in ages and was shocked at his gaunt appearance. Charlie used to be a buff, outdoorsy type. Now his shoulders sagged in a loose shirt with none of the former musculature that made even ordinary clothes look finer. I anticipated that at some point in the conversation he would reveal a cancer diagnosis. Consequently, I was taken off guard when he responded to my question.

"So, how are you doing, Charlie?" I asked, taking a sip of the latte. It was super-hot.

He shook his head. "You ever have a dream just blow up in your face?"

My eyebrows bunched.

"I moved into my dream house a few months back, only the dream has turned into a nightmare," he said.

"Oh?"

"Inherited my uncle's old farmhouse, gorgeous place with lake access, not far from the Daniel Stowe Botanical Gardens. A marvelous old stone house with a front porch, fireplace, and lots of out buildings…" He laughed then, but it was an edgy laugh, not one filled with ha-ha.

"Sounds great," I said. "Did it turn out to be a money pit? Bad roof? Termites? Plumbing issues?" I took another sip of my drink. It was at the perfect temperature now.

"*That* I could handle." He waved me off. "Nah, nothing like that, the house is solid…"

"But?"

He waved again. "I don't want to bore you with my crazy shit. What's up with you? I heard you and Roger finally got married. About damn time." His cheery voice was forced, he would not meet my eye. I followed his downward gaze to his hands and noticed a nervous twitch in his fingers. He gripped his cup, the tremor stopped. Not cancer then, maybe Parkinson's, I thought.

Back in our school days, our group of friends had nicknamed Charlie "Eeyore", after the pessimistic Winnie-the-Pooh character. He was affable and funny, but his humor had always had a defeated, see-that's-what-you-get edge. He saw life in shades of gray and black. At first this evoked my inner cheerleader who wanted to show him the sunny side and put a positive spin on his views. We dated briefly, and I had loved him to some degree, but ultimately his cup-half-empty attitude drove me away. Away to Roger who had been waiting in the wings. Roger's charismatic, easy-breezy manner reminiscent of Bill Murray's irreverent character in *Ghost Busters* was a huge draw post-Charlie.

I was sorry to see this shriveled version of Charlie's former self.

There was obviously something bothering him, but I decided to give him some scope, some time. I told him about my marriage and new job at the VA hospital. He nodded, gripping his cup.

Then I turned the conversation back again.

"So, how are you doing? You seem stressed and frankly, you

look like you've been through a...bad time. What's up?"

He made a face and rolled his coffee cup between his hands.

"Oh, come on, you can tell me. Remember? I'm good with secrets, and boy I had to hold in quite a few back in the day."

"You'll think I'm nuts." He had a sudden eye tick that seemed to yank his head to the left along with his left eye.

"Try me."

"Do you believe in ghosts?"

"You know I do! Remember that awful séance I didn't want to go to, and how the planchette raced around until it flew off the Ouija board and hit the wall? You had to walk me back to my dorm after that!"

"Yeah..." Charlie grinned, "Remember when Roger and I got you good in the graveyard? You jumped a mile when I jumped at your from behind that tombstone!" His eye went spastic again.

"Yeah. I almost had a heart attack, you bastard. I swear I stopped breathing for a sec."

His grin faded, his voice grew distant. "Well, we were idiots back then."

"Tell me. What's going on?" I asked, not sure I wanted to hear the answer.

He took a deep breath and exhaled. "Here goes. My perfect farmhouse was part of a poultry farm. It once had a huge barn with chickens and turkeys, kind of a local, small scale outfit, and I'm not proud to say that my uncle wasn't a very nice man, and poultry isn't a very fun profession. I've done a little research..." He took a sip of his coffee and swallowed. "Male birds don't taste as good, so male chicks get killed right off the bat. That alone is pretty gross, really. I think they just crush them or something hideous. Anyway, my uncle kept a couple out for show, especially around October and November so passers-by would see strutting turkeys and want to buy one for Thanksgiving."

"Good advertising."

"Exactly. But even hens can get aggressive. And it's not surprising that when you have a lot of birds in close quarters, they get testy…crazy really. And dealing with agitated birds can make even a kind-hearted person lose his temper. They peck and make a hell of a racket. The noise can make even a deaf person lose his mind."

I nodded. "So…"

"Well, it seems that over the years my uncle got a reputation for being, ah, rough. Abusive. Hitting, kicking, throwing the birds. This only aggravated the chickens and turkeys making them more neurotic and aggressive."

"You started by asking me about ghosts… are you saying you have ghost *chickens* haunting you?" I asked with a smile.

He looked me in the eye as if calculating whether or not to disclose the rest of the story or bolt for the door.

He exhaled. "Yes."

"Just one or…?"

He laughed again. "One would be a piece of cake. Do you know anything about ley lines?"

"I've heard of them. The magnetic lines around the globe, making some places like Stonehenge have extra energy, right? Druids and such were drawn to these places?"

"Right. Well, there's a ley line that runs into Charlotte, and it seems to run right through the farm."

"So, it has more weird energy?"

"Yes. Plus, the farm was on an Indian settlement. A settlement that was attacked and destroyed by vengeful white men in retaliation for the rape of a young woman."

"So…what are you saying, you are haunted by chickens *and* Indians?"

"I'm saying that there is a magnification of heavy energy."

"How does it manifest?" I asked, hoping to keep the skepticism out of my voice.

"All sorts of ways." He tapped the table with his fingers. "If I go for a walk, I hear flapping and crashing in the trees nearby, but see nothing. I hear that *wibble-wibble-wibble* sound that turkeys make. I wake up to roosters crowing, only there are no roosters. When I get out of my car at night and walk to the house, my ankles get pecked and clawed. Look."

Charlie shifted around the table and pulled up a pant leg revealing faded and fresh linear scars at the bottom of his calf. It suggested repeated claw marks.

"Oh, wow." I said.

I pulled back from the table a bit, feeling confused. I'd been out of touch with Charlie for a while and although he had been normal and solid when I knew him, he was sounding like some of my VA patients. For all I knew, he made those marks himself like a cutter, although cutters usually sliced their forearms. He wasn't a druggie when I knew him, but it could be anything. Drugs, late onset of schizophrenia, a psychotic break. He seemed like good old Charlie, just…haunted.

What if he was telling the truth? I felt a chill run up my spine. "Look" I said pointing to my forearms with a nervous laugh. "You've given me chicken skin." It's what my Mom had called goosebumps.

Charlie pursed his lips. My effort at a joke had backfired. "Go ahead. Laugh. Listen, I'm sorry I brought it up—" He shifted as if to get up.

"No, wait. Don't go." I put a hand on his arm. "Sit. Has anyone else experienced what you are describing?" I asked.

"Yes. In fact…" He laughed that ironic laugh again. "In fact, my new neighbor told me shortly after I moved in that he was surprised someone was going to occupy the place. He kept eyeing me like I was a complete fool."

"But that could be anything."

He pulled back and stared at me. "What I mean is, my neighbor told me he knew it was haunted. He's had activity at his house too. I haven't told you the half of it."

I shrugged. "There's probably a logical explanation."

Charlie smacked his hand flat on the table. "No!"

I jerked, almost spilling my coffee.

He leaned forward. "Tell you what. Can you two come out this weekend? Come see for yourself. I *dare* you."

When we were in college, the dare was a favorite ploy Charlie and Roger used to get me to go along with whatever plan they'd concocted. It always worked.

"Fine. I'll talk to Roger. I don't think we have any plans."

Charlie smiled for the first time. "I'll send you directions. Why don't you come for dinner?" He chuckled. "Hope you're okay with vegetarian."

He jotted down his address and phone number on a napkin and we said our goodbyes.

He had barely touched his coffee.

As I said, my husband, Roger is an easy-going, up-for-anything kind of person, and when I related the story of Charlie's haunted farm, he jumped on it.

"How could we pass that up?" Then he laughed. "Are we taking an appetizer? Turkey and cheese flatbread? Chicken wings?"

I smacked him on the shoulder. "No. Vegetarian."

Late that Saturday afternoon, we dressed and drove out of Charlotte. Roger and I had no trouble following Charlie's directions; the drive to his house was pleasant, the weather was cool and clear; there was little traffic. As there was no direct way to get to his house from ours, our route involved short runs and lots of turns. We enjoyed watching a tiny plane land in front of us at Fly Carolina Aviation, and held our breath passing the Evergreen Cemetery. My mother had made me do this whenever we passed a cemetery to prevent a ghost from attaching as we drove past. While I didn't really believe in it, I always enacted the ritual anyway. We passed a small dairy, a tractor repair shop and a Jiffy store advertising FRESH BAIT. We finally found his dirt road and made our way around the potholes to Charlie's haunted dream house.

It did not look haunted.

In fact, it was charming. The yard was freshly mowed; the air smelled of fresh cut grass. The stone house and fenced yard looked like a Currier and Ives print, down to the hand-operated well pump surrounded by flowers. Charlie came out and waved from the porch. Roger carried a bottle of Merlot; I followed balancing a tray of asparagus rollups.

"Hey guys, glad you could make it." Charlie said.

Roger walked ahead of me and did that male-bonding hand shake, shoulder check thing with Charlie. I noted a fleeting look of shock on his face too, not prepared for Charlie's wan presentation.

I was almost to the porch when I heard a flapping sound and something heavy slammed into the back of my leg. A stab of pain shot down the back of my ankle. I stumbled and turned to see what had hit me, almost dropping the appetizer tray.

There was nothing behind me.

But I heard a gibber of chucks and clucks and a *wibble-wibble-wibble.*

Roger turned to me, "Are you experiencing a gravity flux?"

"No. Something hit me."

"There's nothing there, hon."

"Well, something jabbed at the back of my leg. Look."

I turned my leg and glanced down to see two bright red scratches at the bottom of my leg.

"Welcome to my new house," Charlie said. His left eye did a drastic head yanking twitch.

I scampered up to the porch and had another look at my leg. A thin stripe of blood was oozing through the puffy red marks.

"Whoa!" Roger said when he got a look at it.

I was relieved to move inside with the screen door slamming shut behind us. Charlie took the bottle and tray to the living room and set them on a coffee table made from an old trunk.

"Be right back with something for that leg," he said, going to the bathroom and returning with a wet cloth. I accepted it and blotted at my calf. The cold water felt wonderful against the sore spot.

"You see, I told you," he muttered, taking back the cloth.

He led us on a brief tour of the downstairs: a cozy living room with a plain mantle over a generous fireplace with a giant flat screen television suspended above it. The dining room showcased a classic old farmhouse wood dining table with rustic chairs with plump cushions. An oil painting of a work horse in a barn hung on one wall while the opposite wall was mostly picture window looking out on an assortment of bird feeders and a tiered concrete fountain.

"This is awesome, Charlie." Roger said, looking around, eyes coming back to the television screen.

"I know. Thanks. I'll be right back. Make yourselves comfortable." We sat down in the living room while Charlie disappeared into the kitchen.

What struck me was the starkness of his furnishings. When I had known Charlie, his rooms were full of random stuff: salvaged items in need of repair, tools, feathers he had found in the woods, fishing magazines and stained coffee mugs. There were no stacks or haphazard piles. There was almost nothing on the walls or mantle. This just wasn't Charlie.

"You didn't hear anything?" I whispered to Roger.

"When?"

"Outside, when I was attacked."

"Uh-uh. What'd you hear?"

"There was a flapping sound, then chatter."

Charlie emerged from the kitchen with wine glasses, plates and napkins. "These look great." he said, eyeing my appetizers.

"Thanks," I said.

"Forgot the corkscrew," Charlie said as he walked back to the kitchen.

I heard a hard tap at the top of the window that made me jump. Cardinals are known to attack windows, slamming their heads into the pane repeatedly, but this was no cardinal! Far heavier and forceful, the tap sounded like a beak, but the thud was like a basketball slamming the house. The window shuddered.

Roger's eyes snapped to the window. "What the *hell*?"

The window was struck again lower down. Even though it was twilight, there was still light enough to have seen out the window, yet I had seen nothing even though I was looking directly at it. Only the window bowing, taking the impact.

"You heard that, right?" I said, my voice weak.

"What *was* that?" Roger asked, standing up and moving to the window.

"A poultrygeist," Charlie said, re-emerging from the kitchen with the corkscrew.

Roger growled, "Dude, are you nuts? How can you be so cool? Something almost busted your window!"

Roger was peering out the window looking all around for the culprit. "I don't see anything. I expected to see a dizzy turkey or some kid's toy. Do you have neighboring rug rats screwing with you?"

"No. You are wasting your time. You won't see anything. It's best to just ignore it," Charlie said, working the corkscrew into the cork.

"*What*?" Roger and I asked simultaneously.

I heard the faint sound of chatter again, *wibble-wibble-wibble* followed by another scratch and slam, this time low. The thud was not as forceful this time, but I still jumped.

Charlie said, "I've already replaced the window once. I'm not sure how many times the insurance company will cover the same vandalism damage." He poured three glasses of Merlot and raised his glass. "Let's have a toast. To old friends and new beginnings." His voice was disingenuous, and he didn't look either of us in the eye.

Like an automaton, I clinked my glass with theirs and took a sip. We settled in to the appetizers. Well, Roger and I did. I noticed that Charlie took some onto his plate but did not try them.

Roger caught my eye. If Charlie hadn't been such a good friend, I'm sure we would have made excuses and left. I could see Roger contemplating options as well but coming to the same conclusion. Was there a way to help Charlie? Was there still a rational explanation? A solution?

I took a gulp of wine and swallowed. "Well you've sure cleaned up your act, Charlie," I said, glancing around again. "You used to be a regular Clutter Man. Always bicycle gears on the table getting greased or a lamp getting rewired. Are you sure you live here?" I asked, in an attempt to be playful.

Charlie looked around. "Yeah. Well. I had to get rid of a bunch of stuff. It was too much always cleaning up, re-hanging. I learned that it's just easier to not give them any ammunition."

"What *are* you talking about?" Roger asked.

"Well, magazines flapping around like angry ghost-swans is one thing. Getting knocked out by a remote control pitched like a baseball is another. I spent a whole winter painstakingly gluing together a model of the USS Constitution only to watch it get hurled into the fireplace and burned like lighter pine. I had an antique Swiss Colonial clock, you know the kind with the gold balls that spin around in a glass dome? I ducked just in time on that one, it was coming straight for my heart. I still have a mark."

Charlie hoisted up his shirt suddenly revealing a bruise the size and color of an Idaho potato along his ribs. He laughed again. "I thought I'd saved it that time too. I righted it and by a miracle it looked like it was going to work still. But the next morning I found it in a dishpan in the sink, full of water."

Roger said, "Damn, Charlie! If that's true, why are we here? Why are you still here?"

Charlie ran both hands over his head. "When I found out I inherited this house, it seemed like a dream come true. I don't get lucky. I don't have gifts showered on me. I drove out here and cried, got down on my knees and cried with gratitude this place is so beautiful. The first few weeks were just great. I moved in, painted, did some cabinetry in the kitchen. It felt so good. But then the weird started. Subtle stuff at first. Sounds. Thumps. Noises when there shouldn't be noises. Then things moving around. Couldn't find stuff when I knew it should be there. Stuff like that."

A blaring fire alarm went off in the kitchen. We all jumped.

"Shit!" Charlie exclaimed, rushing toward the kitchen. We heard an oven door creak open and smelled a whiff of smoke. "Shit, shit, shit, you bastards!"

Roger and I rose and trotted to the kitchen.

I gasped.

There were feathers all over the floor. The oven door was open, gray smoke billowed out, and Charlie was pulling out a pan containing charred unidentifiable cubes. He dumped the pan on the stove and shut the oven door with a foot.

"I am so sorry. You see, I stupidly thought, hoped, really, that because you were here, it would keep them away. All would be normal, I'd have no witnesses. You see, I'm not making this up. It's a small comfort, really, in the midst of this culinary disaster."

Charlie coughed and tossed off the oven mitt he'd been wearing. He parked his hands on his hips. "I should have known better, I should have stayed here and watched. Look." He pointed to the oven dials. "I set it on 400 degrees and Bake. Now it's on the highest temperature and Broil." We covered our noses and breathed through our mouths. My eyes were feeling scratchy from the smoke already. I glanced at the dials and stepped back.

BROIL. It was true. The gears in my mind were stuck as logic and fear fought for territory. Had we had a good view of the kitchen before? Not really. Could he have done all this himself? Was he mad? Or was the house really haunted by something malevolent? Either way, the urge to run screaming out to the car was strong.

A white feather floated down from the top of the refrigerator.

Wibble-wibble-wibble!

I jumped again as something soft and feathery tickled against my leg. I assumed some bird was in the kitchen and had brushed past me, but there was nothing there.

Wibble-wibble-wibble! The sound moved out of the kitchen into the dining room.

In disbelief I followed the retreating sound. Turning the corner into the dining room, I stopped and screamed. The couch was turned around and pushed up against the wall. All the cushions were stacked in the center of the room.

Roger and Charlie came up behind me.

"Holy shit!" I said.

"That's new." Charlie said.

"That does it, we've seen enough," Roger said. "We're outta here. Charlie, you're coming with us. Do what you gotta do, lock doors, turn off whatever. Let's go. We aren't leaving you here."

I was on the brink of an intensity of fear I had not experienced since childhood. Hearing the near-panic edge to Roger's voice, amplified my terror. Roger, Mr. It's-All-Good was afraid too.

"No, really, I'll be okay..." Charlie started to argue without much conviction.

Roger propelled us out the door to our car. "Get in."

Roger drove. I sat silent beside him, Charlie was in the back seat. We did not speak for miles. The evening had had such a snowball effect, I hadn't noticed how queasy I had been feeling. As we drove, my stomach relaxed. I looked in the rear-view mirror. Charlie was just staring straight ahead at nothing.

Roger spoke first. "Let's go to Pinky's. Okay with everyone?"

We nodded.

We picked at our food. Criminal, really, the food at Pinky's is outstanding, and I knew some part of me was hungry, but when I brought the fork to my mouth, I just couldn't do it.

Roger spoke softly. "So, you said it escalates. Does it have a regular pattern? What happens next? When does it stop?"

"Oh, it varies. Lots of flapping, cackling…running animal footsteps outside the house, then inside. I've often had feet run over my body while lying in the bed, toenails poking little prick holes into my stomach and legs. The cackling gets louder, deafening, really. Feathers. Lots of feathers. Objects move about as if bumped by flying birds, and blood spatters appear on the walls sometimes. So much blood…But then it all goes away, too. Sometimes it cleans itself as if nothing happened. That's why I didn't think anything would really happen tonight…"

Roger sat back. "Charlie? You can't stay in this house."

"No...no, I guess not." Charlie said as if from very far away. He pushed the food around on his plate but barely ate anything.

Charlie mumbled that he felt that he deserved the haunting as a karmic cleansing, he was being punished for something he did in this life, another life, or to pay for sins of his family. We tried to dissuade him from these thoughts of self-persecution, but he did not seem to listen. He poked at his baked beans with his fork.

He stayed with us that night and was virtually catatonic the next morning. He was placed in a psychiatric hospital and diagnosed with a severe anxiety disorder. It was about seven months later that I got a letter from him.

Dear Janie and Roger,

An old-fashioned letter, eh? Only choice here really, too remote for phone and don't have a computer. I'm in Alaska! Therapist suggested long vacation in nature. Came to fly fish and couldn't leave. I think this is where I'm meant to be. You'll never believe what happened! While I was in the psyche ward, two square suits came to visit. They were from a huge development firm wanting to buy up land along the river. Offered me a heap for the house! Guess what they want to do with it? Put in a golf resort! Crazy huh? I pretended to be a hold out and they offered more!

I will be forever in your debt. If it hadn't been for you, I'd never have left and the house would have eventually killed me. I feel sure of that now. I didn't realize how close to madness I had become. It's like the house was grooming me, amping up the abuse then slacking off a bit so I would question myself. Had it really been that bad? Was it my imagination? Did I somehow deserve it? Had I locked myself out of the house or had it really locked me out? I'd beg it to let me back in, you know? Then it would scald me in the shower and rattle the bed all night.

The developers thought I'd make a fuss when they described how they were going to tear the house down and all the outbuildings. I could hardly keep the glee out of my voice to tell them that I understood! Sometimes, you just have to let go, right? Ha ha!

I passed through Juno and saw a great house for sale. No worries, not a farmhouse and no birds. Just a happy, young, golden retriever. The owners have had the house for generations and reported that the only reason they have to sell is because they wanted to downsize. The last kid just got married, and it's getting too much for them. They gave me a tour and I got a really good vibe. Lots of stuff about — knitting needles in a basket, knickknacks everywhere, antique guns on the mantel. No way have they had a poltergeist! I watched the dog go from room to room. It didn't react to anything, no reluctance to enter or anything. Safe!

Ride's honking out front. Gotta run. Simply gorgeous day here, you can't believe the air!

Love,

Charlie

My sister came to visit last week. An avid gardener, she begged me to go to the Daniel Stowe Botanical Gardens with her. On the way back, I couldn't stop thinking about Charlie's dream house and the freaky evening there. I asked if we could take a detour, but did not explain why, just that I was curious to see what had happened to the farmhouse of a friend.

The terrain was so vastly different, I was convinced I had made a mistake. But then above a tump of weeds I saw the huge sign:

COMING SOON!
TURKEY RUN GOLF COURSE AND ESTATES
EXCLUSIVE VILLAS IN A GATED COMMUNITY

Bulldozers had levelled everything. The houses, outbuildings, gardens and trees were all gone. The ground had been molded into rolling hills for a future golf course. There was a large weedy retention pond where the neighbor's garage had been. Wide roads had been paved that led to nowhere. Only one structure stood: a skeletal model home for the promised housing development. The concrete floor had been poured, fat beams met forming a vaulted ceiling, with signs of an intended staircase to the second floor. No windows or walls. Weeds. A sunbaked portable outhouse stood where a driveway was staked out. It leaned slightly to the left, the door ajar.

"Wow. Looks like they lost funding or something. Why would they just quit building all of a sudden?" my sister asked.

"Hmm."

A lone cattle egret came in for a landing on the edge of the retention pond.

"There is something weird here, isn't there? It's eerie how *abandoned* it feels," she said.

I heard a faint *wibble-wibble-wibble!* The egret seemed to hear it too, because it jumped and took off. As its legs tucked back in full flight position, I noticed that its undercarriage was dark red, and I could have sworn I saw red droplets falling back into the pond. The pond that rippled with a heavy layer of something thick and dark. I heard Charlie's voice in my head saying in that detached voice, "*...so much blood.*"

I blinked hard and looked again. The egret was all white again, the pond ripples were normal. Not thick red.

I shuddered and pushed the gear shifter so hard towards "D" that I heard it crack. I made a U-turn running off the road into the dirt in my haste. Back on solid pavement again, I hit the gas.

A motion in the rear-view mirror caught my attention. I glanced back at the model home and at the apex of the roof, spotted a glowing white rooster, standing tall and proud. He flapped his wings as if in triumph, then leaned forward in a fully-extended crowing posture, like a petulant, undead weather vane. And although we had the windows up and the air on, I heard the unmistakable, "*Er-*

er, er-ERRRRRR!"

The drive home seemed to take forever. My body felt as if I'd been packed in ice. Despite it being late summer, I sat in the hot tub for a very long time.

Like Charlie, I've become a vegetarian.

Note

This story was a last-minute addition. I just read Tomes of Terror, Haunted Bookstores and Libraries by Mark Leslie*. This story is derived from an event briefly described as happening at the Reid Memorial Library at the Lewis and Clark Community College in Alton, Illinois.

*published by Dundurn Press, Toronto, Ontario, Canada 2014. (Page 108)

See Ya

I was on vacation when Dream (yes, that's her name) was interviewed and hired for the part-time job. A good thing for her, really, as I prefer young men to young women as co-workers. Less chatty, less fussy. Particularly with the millennials and their oversharing. Do I lose sleep over which version of iPhone she really, really wants? No. Do I want to see a picture of her lunch? No. Do I wonder why her boyfriend hasn't responded to her text with the photo of her lunch sent over ten minutes ago? No.

Do I expect her to focus on her job, be accurate and responsible? Yes, I do.

But like I said, I wasn't here when she started the job, and I didn't get the chance to screen her, or brief her.

I've been here at the Philomena Bain Lippincott Library for over thirty-five years now, and I've noticed that there are three camps regarding the ghosts here.

Those in the first camp either simply do not draw the attention of the spirits or are in utter denial of the odd phenomenon that they witness. For them, the ghosts do not exist and all talk of them is quashed.

Those in the second camp *have* experienced otherworldly events and find it charming; a perk of the job to have first-hand stories to tell...

Those in the third camp are frightened so far out of their comfort zone that they leave and never return. We've lost quite a few that way. One girl had an encounter in the ladies' room with a phantom in a top hat. She ran out forgetting her purse. When I called her to come retrieve it, she refused to come inside; I had to meet her on the front steps.

It's a touchy subject to broach with a potential new employee. I mean, I've thought about making up a questionnaire, but honestly, what would the questions sound like? "So, are you comfortable being alone in a room with a hostile apparition? Do you mind picking up books that have been thrown at you? How do you think you would respond to a practical joke from the Other Side?"

But I would have hinted to Dream that she might experience... unusual things. I would have given her fair warning.

But she was interviewed by Fergus Whelan, the library supervisor firmly footed in the camp of denial.

Fergus is older than I am and suffers some hearing loss, a weak stomach and a trick knee. He retains the general build and posture of a military veteran and is a consummate gentleman. His Irish accent becomes more pronounced when he's tired or aggravated.

Fergus has been here for ten years and in all that time has managed to explain away the flickering lights as an old wiring issue, the eerie voices as quirks in the air vents or a sporadic hiss from the water fountain. The phantom people often seen in the stacks he chalks up to a trick of the light. Even being locked in the break room repeatedly, he attributes to a sticky door. Humidity. Age of the building.

I almost envy him his position. He shuffles about contentedly in the evenings while the rest of us get jumpy and tend to eye the clock for the time when we can leave the building for the night.

Dream was assigned to me on my first morning back from my Caribbean cruise. I was to give her an idea of how returned books are organized on carts for the volunteers to re-shelve. To her credit, she was well groomed, prompt and eager. She was more reserved than I had expected. As I gave an overview of her new duties, she nodded. Good eye contact. No eye rolling or sighing like some newbies I've had who cop the attitude that it's all beneath them. This one might work out, I thought.

It was first thing Monday morning, and I'll confess, I was still working some rum punch out of my system. Part of me was still gazing over a massive buffet trying to decide, salmon or prime rib? Mashed or scalloped potatoes? And wasn't the guy carving the meat a hunk of goodness? *Mmm, mmm!*

We had pushed two loaded carts into the elevator and had gotten off on the third floor, adult fiction. We stepped away from the carts so I could give her a tour of the floor. We crossed to the reading room where I gave her a rundown of the newspapers and magazines.

"You wouldn't think it would be an issue, but the newspapers especially never seem to get put away properly. You may find them on the floor, or scattered across the tables. Take a moment to tidy them and put them away."

I wasn't quite ready to explain that the human readers weren't the only untidy ones. But I started down that road of disclosure.

"Do you know the history of this library?" I asked.

"Some. I know that it was a private library originally, but the state took it over back in the fifties, wasn't it?"

"Yes, that's correct."

"And it's the largest branch library, and the oldest in the state."

"Yes. Good."

We had just stepped out of the reading room when we heard the elevator whirr to life on its way back down. A metallic clank made us both start and look towards the elevator. There was an insistent hum of the motor trying to work, but the light above the door had gone out.

A woman's muffled voice called out, "Hello? Hello? Oh, please help. I'm frightened."

The hair on my arms rose. The library was not open to the public for another half hour. We'd been the only ones on the elevator coming up, so who was in there trying to go back down?

Dream put a hand to her mouth, "Oh! There's a woman stuck in the elevator!"

We moved quickly to the elevator door.

Dream called, "Hello? Can you hear me?"

"Please help! I'm trapped in here. It's dark, there's no air!" Her voice seemed to be coming from just below the floor level.

We heard an echoey banging as the woman beat on the door.

"What do we do?" Dream asked.

I called, "Try pushing the down button, give it a minute, then try the up button. If that doesn't work, try the door open and closed buttons,"

"It's so dark. I can't see," the voice said.

"Do the best you can, but don't mash them all at once."

"Oh, please help me," she wailed.

"Did you push the buttons?" I asked.

"I think so."

Something about the voice gave me a chill. It sounded hollow.

"The branch manager has an elevator key. Hopefully that will override the jam. If not, we'll have to call the fire department."

"*Please!* Get me out!" The voice called.

"Don't panic. I know it's cramped, but the car isn't air tight. You have plenty of air. Try to stay calm. We'll get you out," I called down. "I'm calling the branch manager now."

"Oh, *please* hurry!" the woman said. Her voice was rising, she was clearly panicked. "The lights went out. It's so dark in here."

I turned to Dream. "You stay here and keep talking to her. I'll phone Ellen."

"You don't have a cell phone?" Dream asked.

"Left it downstairs," I lied. I don't have one. I know, I'm a dinosaur. I just haven't needed one. A widow with no children, I have no one to call.

"Okay," Dream nodded. She put a hand on the door. "I'm here. Please don't be scared, this will just take a few minutes."

I trotted over to the nearest work desk and called Ellen West, the branch manager. The phone rang several times and Tim answered from the information desk.

"Tim, it's Barbara. The elevator is stuck with a woman inside. She's very agitated. Do you know where Ellen is?"

"She was going to be a bit late this morning. Dental appointment, I think."

"Great. Do you know where the elevator key is?"

"Must be in her office. I'll text her for you."

Great. While the rest of the library staff worked in a common room or at desks out in the public space, Ellen, as branch manager had an office that she kept locked.

"Thanks, Tim. I'll try calling her too," I said. I hung up and dialed Ellen's number.

Ellen was a bit on the passive-aggressive side, and as I suspected, my call went right to voice mail. I trotted back to Dream and the elevator.

"Oh thank God you're back," she sighed. "Got the key? This woman is freaking out."

A steady banging mixed with a pitiful wailing reverberated from the elevator.

"I think she's banging on the door with her shoe," Dream said. "I asked her to calm down and try the buttons again, but she's gotten all wigged out."

"Did you ask her what her name is?"

"Yup. She didn't answer me."

"Could be a homeless person. They wander in for the rest rooms and air conditioning, and aren't always the most coherent people." I suggested.

Dream said, "Ah, gotcha."

I gestured for Dream to stand back, and I pounded on the door. "Hello? Can you hear me? We need you to calm down so we can communicate. What is your name, ma'am?"

All sounds stopped. I pushed the up button. Nothing. I pushed the down button. Nothing.

I called again, "Ma'am? What is your name?"

The voice just sobbed pitifully.

"Ma'am, you must stay strong. Please take a deep breath and try to relax. I've called the manager..."

"You don't have the key?" Dream asked, her eyes wide.

In a low voice I said, "The key is in locked in the manager's office. She's at a dental appointment. I've called and Tim texted, but she hasn't responded.

"So, do we call the elevator company?"

"I don't think the elevator company has an office in this town... seems like last time we scheduled servicing, they came from Madison. If we don't hear back from Ellen, I guess I'll have to call the fire department."

Dream's eyes widened. "You know what I don't get is, where did she come from? We were the only ones to come up, right and then the elevator stayed up here..."

"Dream, there's something I think I should tell you," I began, but was interrupted by the phone ringing. I answered it. It was Ellen.

"Barbara? Is the woman still in the elevator?"

"Yes."

"Okay, I'm on my way. Please tell her to hold on, I'll be there in about ten minutes."

"Should we call the fire department?" I asked.

"No, hopefully it won't be necessary. The override should work."

The sobbing from the elevator was taking on a lamenting, mournful tone.

"She's really freaked herself out. She's not responding to us."

"Hmm. I'm on my way."

Ellen clicked off. As I walked back to Dream, I noticed she was holding her phone to the door. I stepped next to her and tried mashing the buttons again. Nothing. I banged a hand on the door.

"Hello? Please hang on. The manager will be here in just a couple minutes."

"Oh please hurry!" the woman wailed. My hand felt cold touching the door; I pulled it back.

"Ah, Dream, I think I should warn you, um, from time to time... odd things happen here in the library, you know it's old and..."

The phone at the desk rang startling me, then strode over and picked up.

"Hey, Barb, Tim. Is the woman still in there? I tried pushing the call button down here, but there was nothing. How about up there?"

"Same. Nothing. You can't hear her? She's crying up a storm and banging on the walls."

"No, but she must be pretty close to you. Uh, the doors open to the public soon. I'll set out the temporarily-out-of-order sign in the lobby."

"Great. Thanks. Ellen said she was on her way. Should be here any minute. She's got the override key."

"Okay." He hung up, but just before I put the receiver down, I thought I heard a thin giggle on the line. It sounded like the voice from the elevator. A shiver flashed up my back.

I looked back at Dream by the elevator with her phone still hovering in her hand. As I walked back towards her, she glanced over at me.

"Any news?"

I hugged myself wishing the chill away. "Tim said he tried pushing the call buttons downstairs, but that didn't do anything."

The pounding began again.

"God I wish she'd stop that. It's so—spooky." Dream said.

"Quite," I said, aware that my neck was tingly.

I called out, "Ma'am, please stop. Would you sit down and rest? Just try to be calm?"

The pounding stopped, the sobbing continued in an unnaturally high mewling.

The desk phone rang again. I walked over and answered it.

"Barbara, it's Ellen. No luck. I turned the key several times, and nothing happened. I'm waiting on a call back from Facilities."

That wasn't good. "Facilities" sounds like an actual department, but in reality it means Woodrow. Woodrow is a stout man in his fifties with unruly gray tufts in his ears, nose and eyebrows and a wide face like a bulldog. While capable, like a government employee, he always lingers on a job longer than necessary so as to appear in high demand. He chats his way in and out of a job reminding people just how in demand he is and that we're lucky he was able to make it out here today. He then rattles off all the other jobs on his list. It is rare that he reports to more than two jobs in a day, regardless of the task, whether changing light bulbs or repairing a toilet. If he did repair a toilet, he'd be done for that day.

"Maybe we should call the fire department as back up? You know how he is."

"Yes. I'm just going to give him a chance to respond."

I sighed. "This woman is crying and bashing on the walls in there."

"I know, I know. Please tell her to hold on."

"Thanks for the update," I said. I hung up.

I went back to Dream again. "No luck. She's calling Facilities, then the fire department."

"Wow. That sucks...I mean, I'm sorry. That's awful."

I pressed my face to the elevator door but recoiled. It was like hugging an ice block. "Ma'am? The fire department will be here in a few minutes. We'll get you out. Please try to calm down."

The thin high voice called back, "Please...*hurry*!" There was such an urgency to her voice...she was either panicking or perhaps had to go to the rest room? This early in the morning, after morning coffee...I've had some mad dashes in my day.

"Hold tight, ma'am. It won't be long now," I called.

I got an echoey sob for a response.

I gestured for Dream to step away with me back toward the reading room.

"What is it?" she asked.

"I don't know how to tell you this, but you know this building is very old and has a long history…and, I don't know if you believe in anything para—"

Just then, the fire door opened and Fergus appeared.

"Hello, ladies," he called as we approached him. "Heard about the elevator. Do we know who the woman is?"

"No," we answered in unison.

"Bad business. Woodrow is apparently replacing a cracked window at the south office this morning, so Ellen called the fire department. They're on the way." He stepped to the elevator and put an ear to the door. I don't hear her. How is she?"

We shrugged.

Fergus called. "Ma'am? How, are you holding up in there?" he called.

"Please…help…me," came the faint high-pitched voice. It put the hair up on my arms.

"The fire department is on its way, we'll have you out in a jiffy," he said. He turned to us. "We've just opened the doors to the public. Hopefully we can get this all taken care of before too many people show up."

Fergus's can-do spirit was a comfort; I felt like hugging him.

Dream's eyes were still wide, taking this all in. I gathered that she felt exhilarated to be saving someone first thing on the job. I wished I could get rid of the sense of uneasiness that was building in me. Something wasn't right about this and I was afraid to give power to my fear.

I touched Fergus's shoulder. "Oh, Fergus, I'm so glad you're here. She's been crying and we feel so…helpless." He gave me a mischievous wink as if this kind of thing happened every day.

That's it, I thought, focus on Fergus. I took a deep breath.

Dream asked, "Does this happen often?" She had a look of excitement in her eyes that struck me as out of place. But, I reminded myself, she's a millennial. No telling what she's thinking.

Fergus answered like a proud father, "No, no, once in a blue moon, is all. No, this elevator has been in steady service for almost ninety years now," He loved this old building.

It seemed an eternity, but finally three burly firemen lumbered through the fire door. "Hullo!"

"Oh, are we glad to see you," I said. I noticed that Dream was still holding her phone in her hand and had been discretely pushing buttons. Taking pictures of the firemen, perhaps? They were young and handsome.

We stood back as they worked a crowbar in the door crack.

In short order they got the doors apart. The elevator dinged. They worked at something in the elevator shaft, and then woosh! The top of the car appeared and moved upwards. The car came level to the floor and opened.

There was no one inside.

My knees got wobbly and I felt unsteady. I had sensed that this would be the case, but the shock still got me. We'd all heard the voice, the pounding and God-awful wailing. Then to see absolutely nothing, well, it was unsettling, so *unnatural.* My vision got blurry and I felt all pins and needles. Suddenly, I was being supported by a strong man, which would have been just heaven but for the various accoutrement attached to his belt poking me in the back.

"Ma'am? Here let's get you a chair. I think you fainted."

"Barbara, are you all right?" Fergus asked, hovering, as the fireman sat me down.

"You saw…there was no one…" I started to say, but my mouth was dry and my head hurt. I swallowed and tried again.

"I'll get you some water," Fergus said and walked briskly away.

Dream patted my shoulder, "Are you all right?"

"Sure. Just a bit of a shock."

The firemen were murmuring together. One stepped tentatively into the elevator car and pushed a button. The door closed, then reopened. *Ding!*

"Okay, I'll try down now," he said and the door closed again.

"Dream. I'm so sorry," I said. "I tried to warn you, you see this building is—"

"Haunted? Oh yes, I know! It's why I was so excited to get this job. Ellen and Fergus told me that state funding is always getting cut, and anything that would bring more patrons to the library to keep the numbers up would be a bonus. Even if it meant a feature in 'Historic Haunts', the new ghost tour company my sister and I started. This is like, the most haunted place in the whole state! I wanted to get a part-time job here to get the day-to-day, first hand experiences, as well as to interview employees and patrons. I never imagined that something this fabulous would happen on my first day! I recorded everything on my phone. I can't wait to play it all back!"

I just stared at her. Didn't see that coming. Not at all.

You know, back in my day, a new employee did not refer to an elder or senior employee by first name, so to hear 'Ellen' and 'Fergus' from this lamb was a bit of a shock. But so was her insinuation that Fergus believed in the ghosts.

I stammered, "But...but Fergus doesn't believe in ghosts. He's been a staunch denier for as long as I've known him...I don't understand."

"That's not exactly true," she said with a grin. "He told me a few stories of things that have happened to him. He just doesn't want to dwell on it. As he put it, it's just 'water cooler fodder'."

Fergus appeared with a glass of water and handed it to me, chuckling. "Yes, in fact, Dream here was so keen on the stories, I thought we could go for happy hour over to O'Hickey's and give her an earful of 'em."

My mouth fell open.

Fergus let out a phlegmy laugh. "Barbara, your face!"

"But...but...in all these years, you've always acted like you didn't believe any of it. You could explain away every flying book, every ethereal voice, even chairs stacking spontaneously."

He laughed again. "Oh, come now Barbara, my name is Sean Fergus Whelan...my family tree on my Mam's side practically built the city of Mullingar. I was raised by wee-men and fairies. I'm about as Irish as you can get! Of *course* I believe in ghosts!" He laughed again until tears formed in his eyes.

"But why pretend then?" I asked, feeling betrayed, lied to all those years.

"Well, you know, Mrs. Sprock, the previous branch manager was a Baptist. She wasn't gonna have any part of ghost story telling. I learnt to keep it to myself and make excuses for when folk got in a tizzy. But now, this whole ghost business has taken off, hasn't it? Ghost channel, ghost tours and the lot. Mrs. West is keen to get more patrons, and it ain't like we have to make it up. I've had nonsense happen in just about every corner of this library." He nodded for emphasis.

And so that evening and for the first time in my employment history, after securing the doors and setting the alarm, the staff of the Philomena Bain Lippencott Library, Ellen, Fergus, Tim, Dream and I wandered down the block to O'Hickey's.

Our drinks arrived. Fergus reached for his Murphy's Stout with both hands and cradled it like a sacred object. Dream ordered a vodka concoction I'd never heard of, Tim had local IPA, Ellen had a Jack and Ginger and I went with a glass of Merlot. The waitress took our appetizer orders. Before she had even pulled her tray back, Dream leaned forward with a tape recorder and asked, "Do you mind if I tape this?"

We all shook our heads no.

"So who was the woman in the elevator? Was that Philomena?"

Fergus took a big swig of beer that left a film on his lip. He swallowed with a sigh of satisfaction, licked his lip and answered, "Likely so."

Ellen said, "Philomena, or Minnie as she called herself, was the daughter of a well-to-do family that made their money from both legitimate and questionable investments, the three 'r's, real estate, railroad and rum running. Minnie was a stunner, a socialite with charisma, the life of the party. With more money than sense, she threw lavish parties and gave away money to various charitable endeavors, including the library. She married twice and died suddenly in her fifties. Her death was shrouded in mystery, as they say, a late night after-party swim gone wrong."

"I'd say so!" Fergus laughed.

"She was found floating naked in a swimming pool at the hotel just across the street there," she pointed out the window.

Tim leaned in, "It was rumored that she was killed and dumped in the pool to look like an accident. Forensics wasn't very good back then. Accident or crime of passion? She was known to have men chasing her, stalking her even."

Fergus interrupted, "Yes, and frequently, you'll walk into the library after opening and find a big puddle of water in the rotunda or at the top of the stairs. Or watery footprints trailing across the hall." He waggled his fingers over the table suggesting the trail of prints.

I remembered the first time I'd found a puddle. Looked at the ceiling, wondered if there were a dog loose in the building, or even if the janitor had peed the floor as some kind of statement. But then sometimes I found watery footprints leading to the elevator door. The air conditioning seemed awfully cold in O'Hickey's. I wished I'd brought a sweater.

Ellen continued, "Minnie was an amateur actress, performing in local theatre productions. Comedies mostly. She had a great sense of humor, but also liked practical jokes. So, unfortunately, the police and fire department are used to coming out for us, like today, only to find that it was a prank."

I said, "But we don't know for sure. It really sounded like there was someone in the elevator. The first time we ignore it, you know we'll get sued by some woman who really was trapped in the elevator."

Dream said, "I know! I thought it was a real person, but I couldn't figure out how she got there. There was no one upstairs when we got up there."

I remembered the voice, "Please...help...me." And the faint laugh in the phone receiver. I took big gulp of wine. I almost wished I'd ordered coffee. I was freezing.

Ghost Lite

Ellen said, "The poltergeist stuff freaks me out."

Tim nodded.

"What's that like?" Dream asked, leaning the slim recorder forward.

Ellen said, "There is a large painting of Philomena on the landing on the second floor. I've walked up the stairs past the painting to go to the rest room, and when I come back, it's upside down. That painting is heavy and is supported by two huge bolts. You have to have two people and a ladder to get that up there. There is no way that a library patron could do that in the time that it takes to use the rest room. It's just not possible." She rubbed her arms. I noticed she had goose bumps too.

"Book stacking." Fergus said, then tipped his beer back and gulped. As he tipped forward again, he pulled out his phone and punched some buttons. Photos appeared on the screen flying past under his finger. He stopped and held up the screen.

"Have a look at that!"

"Wow!" Dream said. "Would I be able to get some of those pics for our website? You'd be credited of course."

"Sure!" Fergus grinned.

"Right," Tim nodded. "Books rearrange themselves. You put the phone down, look up and poof! There's a pyramid of books stacked on your desk. All kinds, like a cookbook, the history of fly fishing and Beatrix Potter…completely unrelated stuff that would have to come from the return desk. And it stacks itself totally silently. No ruffling pages, no thumps, nothing. Turn around and poof! An issue of *Better Homes and Gardens* just appeared in front of your computer screen. "

"Ugh. The computers," I said, suddenly recalling a tortuous day when every search request I typed in came back with a kindergarten teacher guide book called *Quest*. "If she knows you are under stress, she'll make it worse. You have people three deep at the checkout, and the scan machine starts blipping a children's song."

I looked around me at our little group. Dream, eyes wide soaking up the stories like a Bounty paper towel; Ellen, slurping her whiskey, laughing; Tim, leaning forward like a gossip columnist; and Fergus, smiling and radiant. I wanted to go home, take a hot bath, put on my jammies and snuggle with my cat.

"But there are other spirits as well, right?" Dream asked.

"Oh yes," Fergus nodded. "In fact, it's possible that the library is some kind of spirit station. We have our regulars, but then it seems like we get spooks that are just passing through, too." He flipped through more photos and displayed the screen again.

"Get out!" Dream cooed.

Tim leaned forward to have a look. "Great shot!" he said.

Yes, scary things passing through, I thought. Like the skeletal hand that grabbed my ankles in the bathroom stall and yanked. That was a dark thing. Scared me to death. And those cold, cold boney fingers. I felt those cold fingers around my ankles for hours after that happened.

"Like what?" she asked.

Tim answered, "All sorts. Shadows. Whispers. Tappers. We had one spirit for a few years that drove us nuts, tapping on people's shoulders, but of course they'd turn around to confront the rude person and there was no one there."

Fergus half-laughed, half-grunted. "Mind, this sounds like stuff is happening constantly. That's not true. But there is steady activity. Nothing really bad, though, thank goodness. Just annoying and spooky."

"Well the thing that grabbed my ankles was dark," I said, my voice weak. But the waitress arrived with the appetizers and began setting them out. I don't think anyone heard me.

Fergus tossed a jalapeno popper in his mouth and chomped.

Tim tugged at an enormous fried onion.

Dream asked, "What about the Hanging Man. Where is he?"

I was going to put some sweet potato fries on my plate, but my hand hung in the air, the fork hovering over the fries. The hanging man was in the old coat room. I remembered when I first saw him. It was a rainy day in March, one of those dreary days when the library is almost empty because no one wants to go out. I opened the door and saw the man hanging in front of me, eyes bugged, tongue protruding. He wasn't quite dead yet, in fact, there was a terrible gargling sound and his legs were kicking against the wall. He rolled his eyes at me in a helpless pleading look. His face was almost purple. I screamed, and he faded away. That horrid gargling noise was still in the air. I would have run, but I was frozen in shock. I always thought ghosts were filmy. My first impression was that I had interrupted a real man actually hanging himself and I had done nothing. He looked to me for help and I was too frightened to move. Shock, fear, self-loathing overwhelmed me and then it was gone, just like that.

"You saw him, didn't you Barbara?" Tim asked, an eager expression on his face.

I pulled my hand back.

"Barbara? Are you okay? You look pale, you know, ha-ha, like you'd seen a ghost!" Fergus laughed, and patted my arm.

"I did," I said.

Tim was ripping into the onion. Fergus was laughing, his voice too loud for our little nook. Ellen skewered one of the jalapeno poppers and stuffed it in her mouth.

I blinked. What was wrong with me? I liked these people, didn't I? I'd never dreamed we'd socialize like this. It should have been fun, full of camaraderie. So why did I feel like I was witness to a hyena feast? They were relishing these gruesome stories while my stomach was turning sour?

"I'm sorry. I should go. I need to get home," I said, hoping they wouldn't press me into further excuses. I had a panicky feeling that I needed to bolt. Now.

"Oh, Barbara, didn't you want to tell the one about the time Minnie pretended to be you at the desk and then that old duffer couldn't believe it when you walked in the front door?" Fergus laughed, then began to imitate the frightened old man, "but I, but I, but you, but you…"

"Well you just did, I think," I said as pleasantly as I could muster. I stood up and put my bag over my shoulder. "This has been… quite something."

"But Barbara, you didn't get your second glass of wine. It's two for one happy hour, you know," Ellen said.

"No, that's all right. I'm feeling a little tired. Good night all." I fumbled for my wallet and put down some cash towards my drink and the group appetizers.

Dream caught my hand as I passed her. Reminded of the cold hands on my ankles, I fought the urge to yank it back.

"Thanks for today," she said." You were great. So calm. Just great."

"Oh," I shook my head. "Not really."

"See ya," and "Goodnight" they chorused behind me.

I walked briskly back to the library parking lot, avoiding looking at the windows. You never knew what you'd see in the windows. Orbs. Lights. Faces. "See ya," kept echoing in my head.

Thirty-five years.

"See ya, Barbara," Fergus had said. Fergus who pretended and denied it all for ten years to my face and now was laughing and loving the recapping.

"See ya, indeed," I thought as I drove home. I had some sick time coming. I had decided to retire next year anyway. The more I thought about it, the more I never wanted to set foot in that library again.

As I drove out of the parking lot, I rolled down my window and yelled, "See ya, Minnie! See ya, Spooks! See ya, Hanging Man! See ya!" and I hit the gas.

Note

The University of the South is in Sewanee, Tennessee. In my era, the mid-eighties, faculty dogs roamed the campus freely attending classes, going to the movies, sleeping in the roads. Some dogs even got diplomas for fulfilling class hour requirements. Gordon, the Great Dane was banned from Dean Croom's calculus classes for excessive yawning. He really did escort me back from the Memorial Cross.

Blessings to all Sewanee dogs wherever you may be.

There is a legend of a Green's View ghost.

My gifted massage therapist told me a story that was the seed for the rest. Thank you, Ram.

Benevolent Guides

Normally I try to be quiet during a massage, but I hadn't had a session in a long time and was inordinately chatty catching up with my therapist, Asa. The subject of ghosts came up, and I found myself babbling about the ghosts from The University of the South, my alma mater.

"There's a road called Green's View," I said, "that runs along a golf course out to a bluff overlooking a valley. At night you can see the lights from two cities in the valley and the night sky full of stars. With no light pollution, it's a fabulous spot for stargazing. But it's also creepy out there. I went several times, and each time within minutes, a feeling of approaching dread overwhelmed me and I had to leave. It wasn't just me either. I drove out with a friend one night. We parked and studied the sky. Within moments, I began feeling anxious but tried to act normal. However, after identifying several constellations, my friend turned to me and said, "Let's get the hell out of here. Something's giving me the willies.""

Asa said, "Oh, wow. Any idea what it was?"

"The traditional story is that a freshman goes walking out to Green's View alone. On the way back, a Professor wearing a gown appears, and in perfect southern gentlemanly fashion, escorts her back to campus. But when they arrive at University Avenue, he suddenly disappears."

"So, a good ghost, then."

"Yes. But he appears as an escort to protect the girl from the very bad thing that is out there. Only no one seems to know what the bad thing is."

"Interesting."

"Yeah." I laughed, clearly freefall rambling now and unable to stop myself despite the heavenly neck work I was receiving. "The funny thing is, Sewanee used to have dogs on campus. Most of them belonged to the professors and everyone knew them. There was a geriatric Great Dane named Gordon...not a very bright dog, but absolutely huge. I walked out to the Memorial Cross a couple times. The cross is a massive structure overlooking another valley. It lights up at night; you can see it from miles away. It's quite something."

"Relax...you're tensing," Asa said.

"Right. Sorry. Anyway, the cross is down this long dirt road. I went out there one night after a nasty breakup and cried for a long time. On the way back, I started feeling scared, like, you silly cow, what are you doing on this dirt road in the middle of the night? What if the Green's View thing comes out here too? I was spooking myself silly when Gordon the Great Dane appeared out of the woods, sidled up next to me and walked me all the way back to campus. I was so grateful. I felt so safe, he was as big as a pony."

I frowned remembering Gordon and the way he had just appeared. "It was peculiar too. Gordon wasn't friendly, he didn't care about getting petted plus I barely knew him. It was surreal how he just walked right next to me."

"Dogs are very intuitive. Maybe he did sense something out there and wanted to protect you."

"I know, right? I wonder if his ghost is out there escorting people. That would be cool."

"Totally possible. The person might not even know he was serving that function."

Asa waggled my head. I realized I was holding it at an awkward angle to talk. I relaxed into the face cradle.

"What about you?" I asked, "You've travelled all over the place. Any interesting ghost stories?"

Asa gathered up sections of my hair and tugged. Who knew pulling hair could be such a good thing? "Actually, yes. I grew up in India. One day when I was about four, I was in a huge daytime market, all kinds of foods, fabrics, clothes, amulets, chilies, spices, wood carvings… you name it. I must have wandered away from my mother. I remember standing front of a stall loaded with mangoes. I loved mangoes and they were in season."

"Oh, mangoes are the food of the Gods. I love mangoes." I groaned.

"I wanted one desperately but didn't have any money. This older man appeared, a Brahmin. He had a very kind, wise face and eyes that could look right into your soul."

I interrupted, "This ends well, right? You didn't get kidnapped, did you? Please tell me he wasn't a sex offender."

"No, no. He bought me a perfect mango, so ripe, so juicy… he pulled out a small knife and cut it and peeled it. We sat on a curb and shared it. It was the best mango I've ever eaten."

Asa was working on my hand now, pulling the fingers and digging into the palm. I had to focus on not drooling.

"He asked me what kinds of foods I liked and how I liked school. He walked me around the market like the perfect grandfather, patient and kind. He talked to me like I was a grown up, not like a child. He bought me a coconut water, too. Eventually, we left the market and walked into the temple grounds. There we walked around for what seemed like hours. He gave me a tour, explaining all the statues. We made offerings of incense and flowers. It was wonderful. I was so happy to have so much attention."

"Sounds great," I mumbled.

"My mother found me lighting an incense stick and talking, having a conversation. I told her the nice man had been taking care of me. She asked, 'What man?' It was obvious to me what man. He was right there. But at that moment when she said, 'what man', the man disappeared. He was as real as anything, I even held his hand and then suddenly he was gone. "

"Whoa!"

"And then she was shaking me asking me about him. I told her he was tall and old with a kind and wise face and a long beard. He was wearing a long saffron robe and he had feathery legs and chicken feet."

"What?" I asked.

"Yes. I know. Chicken feet. I was a child. It didn't seem strange to me at the time. But his legs had feathers and he didn't wear shoes or anything, he walked on chicken feet."

"Do you think you dreamed the whole thing?"

"No, I was carrying around the coconut water. And there was something else. Look."

I picked up my head and blinked. My face had mashed into the face cradle, I felt like I had Shar-Pei face.

Asa pulled a string of prayer beads from under his shirt. "He gave me this."

The beads looked ancient. The guru bead, or lead bead was a beautiful yellow and blue swirled stone I didn't recognize.

"I told my mother that he bought me a mango and a drink and then gave me these beads. Her eyes got big and she was quiet. She changed the subject, and never talked about it again. She didn't let me go to the market alone after that."

"Well, yeah!"

"Later I found out that it's a fairly common thing…if a Brahmin dies with some kind of unfinished business, he returns as a ghost in the form of a man, but with the legs and feet of an animal to identify him."

"That's kind of weird."

"Agreed. You know I saw him one other time."

"Yeah?" I asked, settling back down in the face cradle.

"My mother and I were in the market, and I saw the man again. He was a good distance away, walking with a little girl. When I tried to point him out to my mother, she couldn't see him, and then I couldn't either. The girl was alone, talking to herself."

"So, is he a ghostly babysitter?" I asked.

"No," he laughed, "more like a spiritual guide. Remember, he took me to the temple and began teaching me all about the temple deities and customs. I think that was his unfinished business. . I think his spirit was stuck in the market place. I have said prayers for him while I am praying on the beads."

"I like the idea of ghostly protectors," I said, "kindly professors, huge dogs…not so sure about the Brahmin with chicken feet though."

"Does the form matter, so long as they are benevolent?" he asked.

I pondered that question for a long time. Perhaps not. Makes me think we don't really know what energies are around us at any given time, do we?

Note

For Leslie and "Roxanne" our unicorn.

A Roxanne Sighting

I moved to Owensville about a year ago and opened a gift shop. A medium-sized town that started with a town square then sprawled in all directions with no particular plan, it's not a destination town, but I like it. In the older section where I've got my store, there are antique shops, some excellent restaurants, a beautiful park, and a museum. We draw a modest crowd of folks from the interstate who take an extended rest stop.

I'd gotten friendly with Maureen, a woman in my yoga class. I was on my way to meet her for lunch at Laurabelle's, her favorite restaurant. I was driving south on 40th Street, when I was distracted by the silver sparkle of a woman on a bicycle heading north. Oddly, the first thing I noticed was her posture. Her back, shoulders and arms were so straight, it was as if her flesh was a natural extension of the bicycle. Perhaps it was due to her head being held so perfectly perpendicular to the ground. Most people tend to look down towards the ground ahead, but this woman was majestic, her gaze straight ahead as if looking into the future.

It was then that I got a good look at her face. She was pretty, but smiling with an unnatural serenity and vapid expression, a creepy clown kind of smile. I wondered how she kept the bike straight since she seemed to be pedaling in slow motion.

Her feet propelled her in kiwi-green flats that matched her clingy V-top that advertised her great bust. She was a D for sure, out of proportion with her otherwise petite body.

The real show-stopper of the ensemble was the blonde wig with silver highlights spun into a beehive that glistened in the sun. Strands of tinsel had escaped and shimmied like fringe on a flapper dress.

As we were about to pass each other, she turned her head and we made eye-contact. She lifted her left hand and gave me the royal wave, a slow wrist twist, the blank expression and unnatural smile fixed on her face.

I pulled my eyes away and looked straight ahead, feeling stunned. I blinked. Shaking off the irrational notion that I wanted to shower, scrub myself clean, I focused on the traffic ahead. She had to be crazy or heavily medicated. Well, if she was crazy, at least she seemed happy. Power to her, I thought, as I drove on.

Maureen was waiting for me at a table outside. The weather was perfect: sunny, not too hot, there was even a breeze. A waiter appeared and took our drink orders.

As we perused the menu, I related what I'd seen.

"Oh," she said, the cheerful expression draining from her face. She leaned forward. "You need to be very careful the next few days."

"What? Why?" I asked.

She pursed her lips as if pondering how to tell me. "You'll think I'm nuts, but I have to tell you…you had a Roxanne sighting."

"Who is she?" I asked.

The waiter returned with our drinks. I unwrapped my straw and stuck it into my lemonade.

"Sometimes the newspaper does stories on her around Halloween time. She's our local legend. She was a dancer and small-time actress who did imitations of people onstage: Marilyn Monroe, Jackie Kennedy, Mary Anne from Gilligan's Island, Dolly Parton …"

"She's got the build for that, for sure." I took a sip of lemonade. "Oh, tart!" I made a face.

Maureen raised an eyebrow.

"I meant the lemonade," I said.

"She got into a drug and party crowd and eventually couldn't keep it together to do her acts…showed up late and high, forgot her lines. That kind of thing. Then she got into something that almost killed her. She was taken to the hospital with some massive overdose, and they were able to save her, but she suffered permanent brain damage. Functional, but childlike. She lost her job, ended up homeless."

The waiter came and took our sandwich orders.

"Well, she looked pretty good, I mean, her clothes were clean, her skin looked like a beauty ad. She's a pretty girl, but that empty expression…gave me the creeps."

Maureen set her tea down. "Well, that's the thing." She bit her lip and stared at the table. "She ended up hooking, and used her former stage outfits. She was seen on 12th Street in all kind of costumes. One of the movers and shakers around town paid for her to have proper housing, but it didn't keep her off the streets. Of course, no telling how much business she got looking kind of spacy all the time."

I grimaced, her image vivid in my mind. "I'm not sure who she was supposed to be today." I said, trying to think of anyone famous for a silver beehive.

"I'm sure sometimes she just went mix and match. This wig, that dress," Maureen said. She balled her hands into fists and pressed them on the table. "But here's the thing, Diane. She died about five years ago, she bicycled right out in front of a beer truck.

Got squashed."

"What?" I asked, choking on lemonade.

"You saw a ghost."

I pulled back from the table and shook my head. "No. She was solid. Plain as day. In the daytime. She waved at me."

"I know. And that's another thing. See, people believe that if you see her, she's warning you about a pending danger. Slow down. Be watchful. People who laugh it off have accidents." She bumped her fists on the table.

"Are you serious?" I said, half expected her to laugh and say, "Ha! You fell for it."

Instead she narrowed her eyes at me. "I had a boyfriend who rode a motorcycle. He saw her looking like Marilyn Monroe in the white dress, you know, where she stood over the grate? The… next…day he was riding along when a little kid ran out in the street, he swerved, and the bike fell. He and the bike skidded for I don't know how many yards. His whole left side was torn up like hamburger. Lucky it wasn't worse."

"Yikes," I said.

The waiter brought our sandwiches, but suddenly I wasn't hungry. It looked delicious, but I knew I wouldn't be able to eat it or enjoy it. I nibbled a sweet potato fry. I'd ask for a box next time the waiter came around.

"Trust me on this," Maureen said. "I've heard of several people who ignored the warning and had an accident. Usually within a day or two of the Roxanne sighting."

I exhaled. Get a grip. Be more careful.

Maureen grabbed her pastrami sandwich, took a big bite and moaned. When she had swallowed, she said, "Wow, this is so good."

"Mm-mm," I said, picking at another fry. "I think I'll save

mine. I seem to have lost my appetite."

"I hope I haven't scared you. You'll be fine if you're careful. My mother had a Roxanne sighting two years ago, I guess it was. That night she was just about to make a left turn, she had the light and all, but a student on a black moped was texting and blew right through the red light. If my mom hadn't paused for a second to make sure that the road was clear, she would have plowed right into her. The glow from the phone screen caught her attention."

Well that was good news, I thought. See? Just be careful.

Our conversation shifted to jobs, kids and upcoming events. I had almost forgotten about Roxanne until I got back in my car and fastened my seat belt. Normally I drive about five miles an hour over the speed limit, but on the way home, I drove like a little old lady. I looked left-right-left-right. I full- stopped at every intersection. Stopped on the stale yellow.

I was vigilant all the next day back and forth to work, to the grocery store. No incidents. A pickup truck roared around me then cut back in front of me. The driver flipped me a bird, annoyed that I was minding the speed limit.

"Fine," I said, as if he could hear me. "Hope you see Roxanne and take heed."

A cold front came through that night, the temperature dropped into the forties with rain, thunder and lightning that came in waves. I lost power for a few hours and had trouble sleeping.

By morning, the angry storms had moved on, but a persistent rain pelted the roof. Driving to work was slow as the road looked like a river with expansive puddles like trout pools. Streams of water gushed into the drainage ditches; lush grassy lawns were becoming ponds.

Although my windshield wipers were thrashing wildly, I got only glimpses of clear view. A truck rambled in the opposite direction dousing my Honda. I might as well have driven into a lake. I eased on the brake and crept forward feeling a play in the road between moments of traction and moments of floating. My fingers hurt from gripping the steering wheel and the rapid *sha-wump sha-wump* of the wipers was not helping my nerves. It was a relief to stop at a red light. Thank goodness I had just a few more blocks to go.

The light turned green. I glanced left-right-left-right and was just about to push down on the gas pedal, but something made me hesitate. To my right, a gray Volkswagen in the turn lane had slowed to stop but lost traction in a puddle and hydroplaned out into the intersection throwing up jet ski-like rooster tails. It skated out in front of me in a pirouette, gliding to a stop two feet from my bumper. Had I stepped on the gas, we would have collided like bumper cars.

Through the watery distortions of our windshields, I saw a round-faced woman in her sixties, hands clenched on the steering wheel. She dropped her head for a moment in what could only be relief that we had avoided a crash. Beyond her, I spotted two occupied child seats.

She was driving her grandchildren to school, I thought.

As the woman steered her car out of the way, I took a deep breath with relief. "Whew! Thanks, Roxanne," I said.

It was probably my imagination, but I heard a breathy Marilyn Monroe-ish voice from the back seat whisper, "You're welcome."

Made in the USA
Columbia, SC
22 January 2024

29862108R00121